MIRACLE MIND

A Course In Miracles Coloring Book

50
Transcendent
Quotes & Images

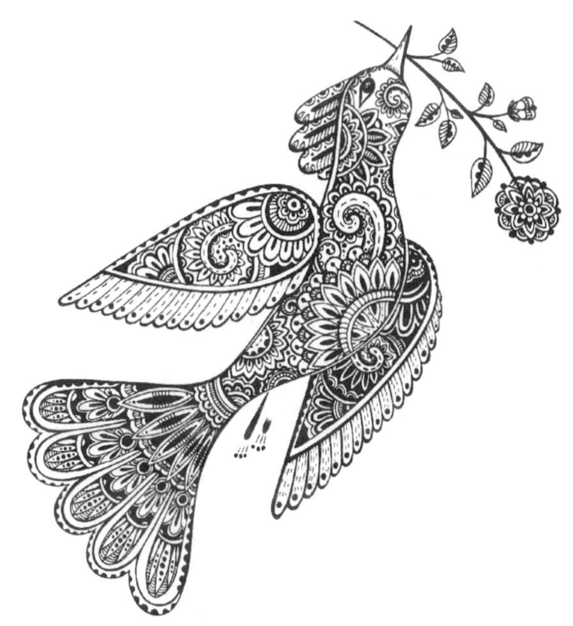

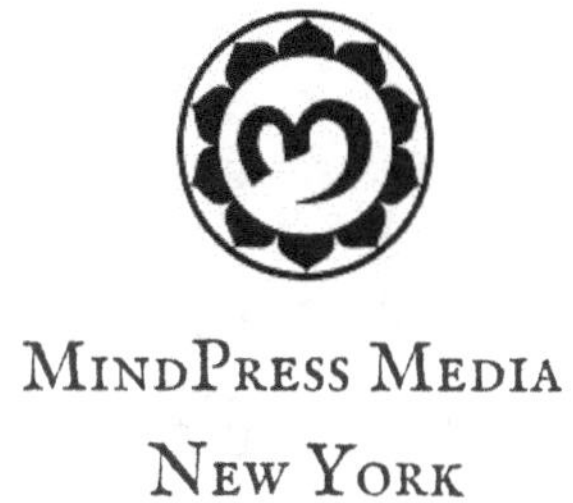

MindPress Media
New York

MindPress Media publishes works that inspire inner transformation
and lead us to perceive the sacred in our world.

32 Fort Greene Place, Brooklyn, NY 11217
www.mindpressmedia.com
info@mindpressmedia.com

Grateful acknowledgement is made to
the Foundation for Inner Peace.

ISBN: 978-0-9894912-3-5

Printed in the United States of America

ALSO BY MINDPRESS MEDIA:

365 *MIRACLES:* Daily Journal Of
A Course In Miracles Workbook Lessons

**We hope you enjoy your coloring experience.
Please leave a book review online and share your artwork!**

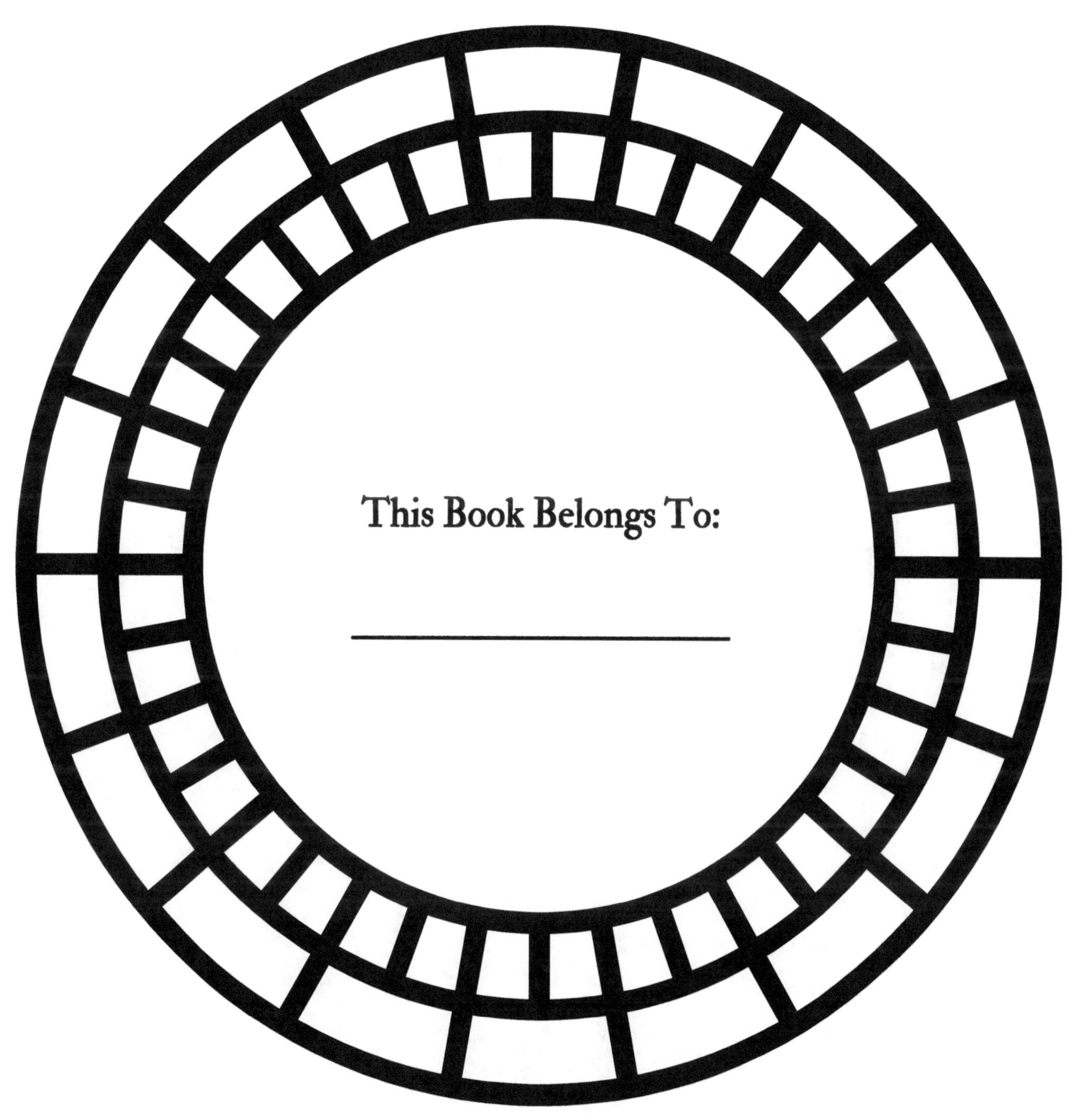

TIP: Use this page to test your coloring medium and palette!

There is no order of difficulty in miracles.

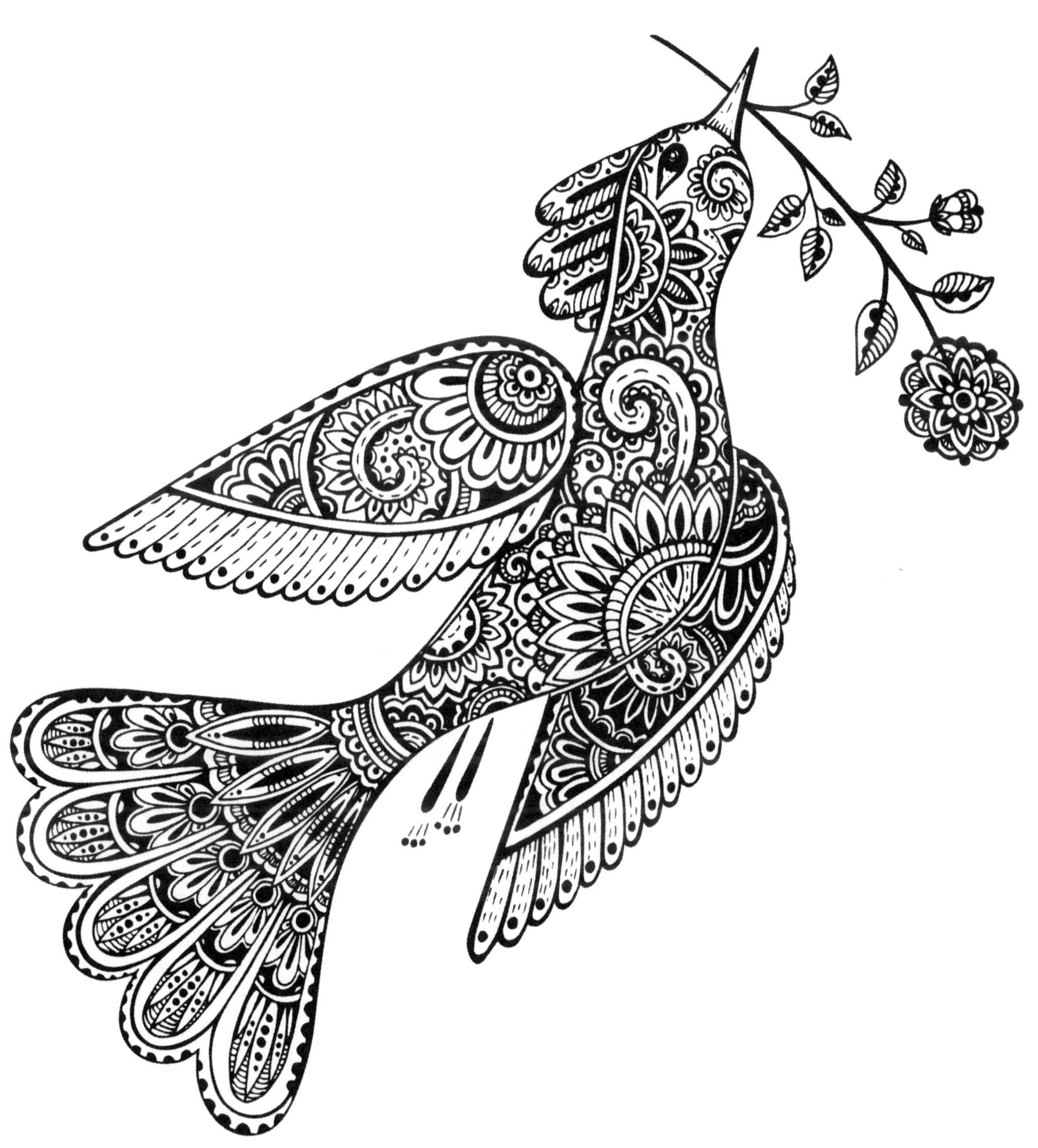

Miracles occur naturally as expressions of love.
The real miracle is the love that inspires them.

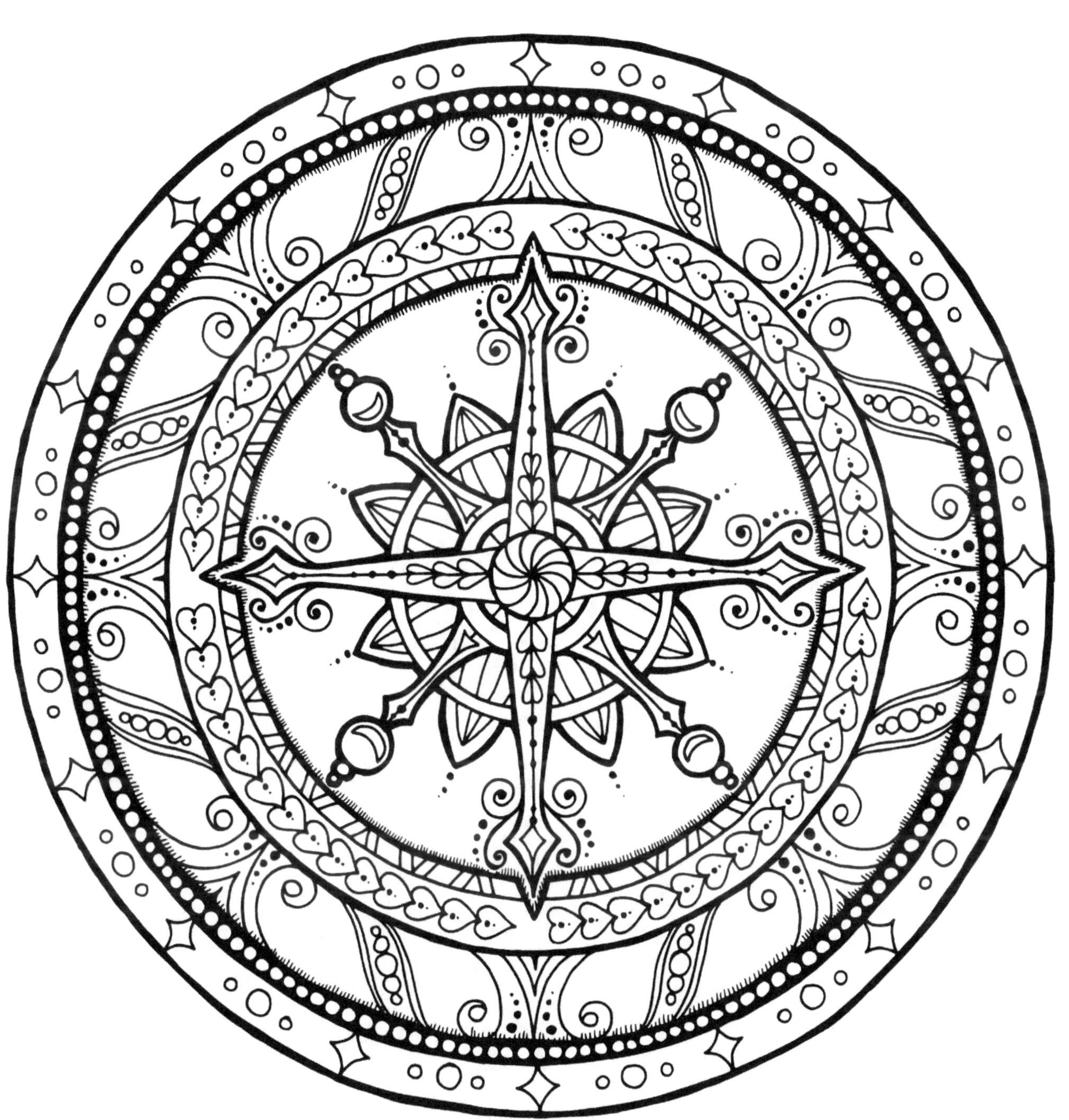

Prayer is the medium of miracles. Through prayer love is received, and through miracles love is expressed.

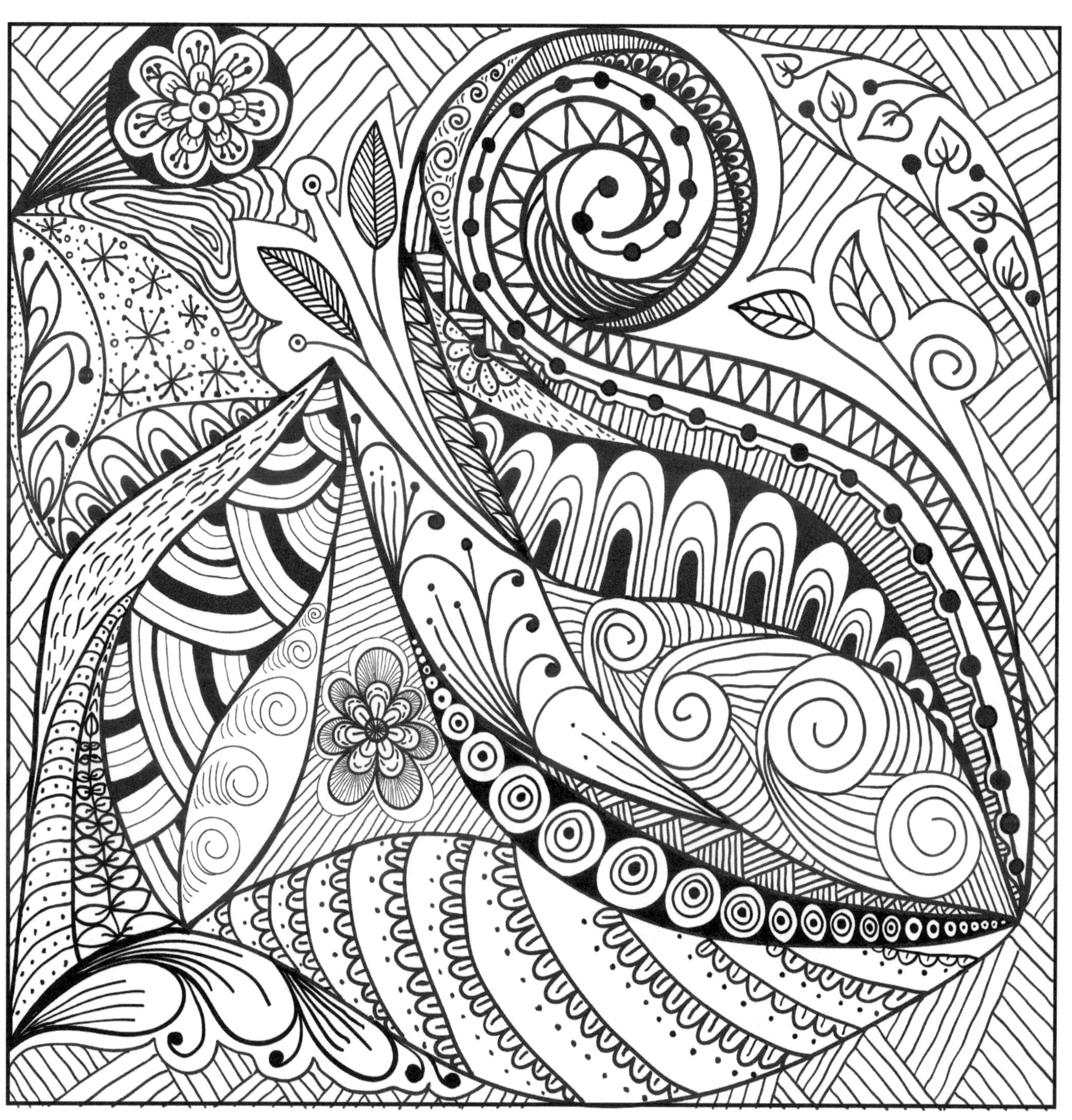

A miracle is *now*.
It stands already here, in present grace.

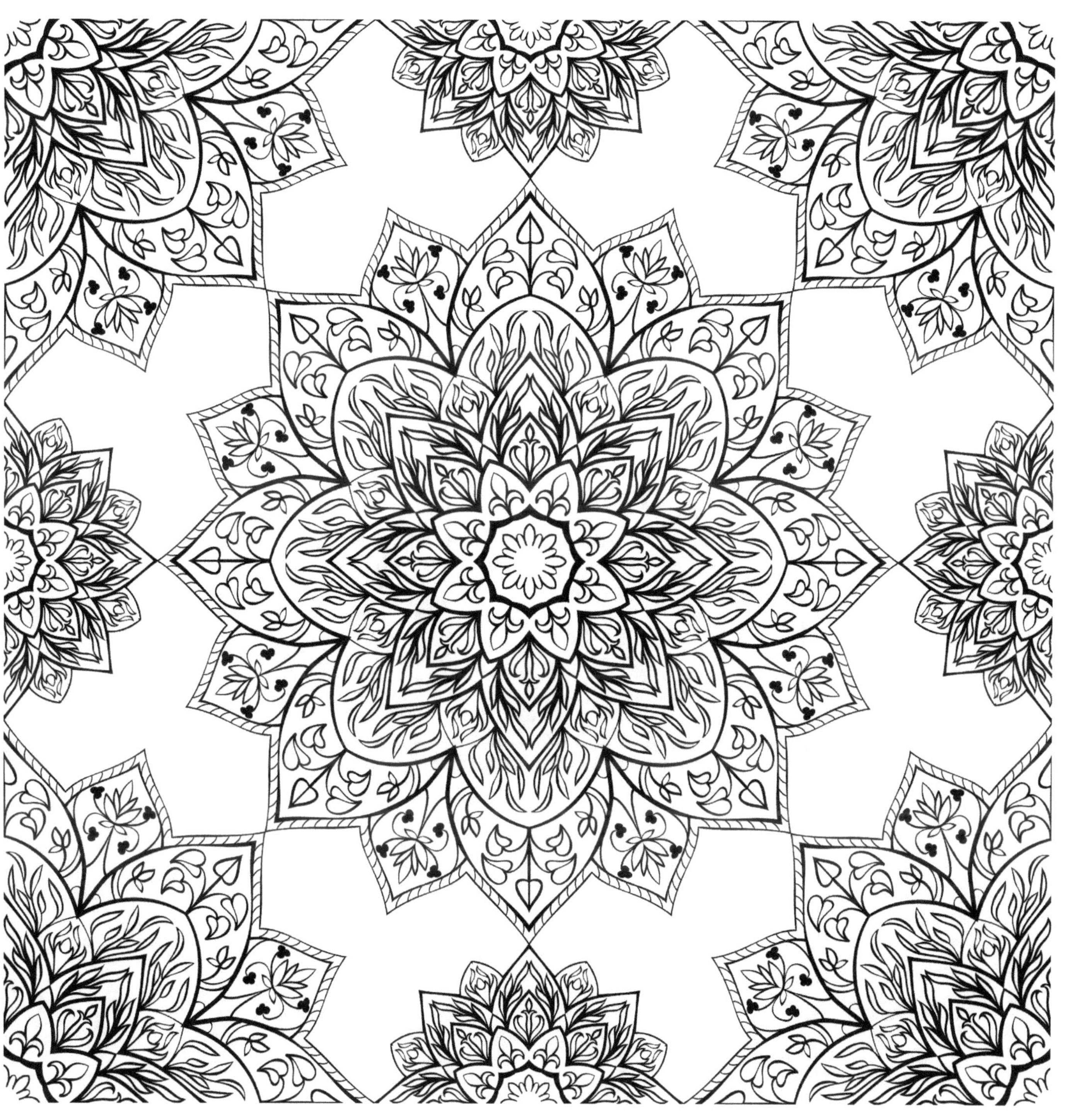

Everything that comes from love is a miracle.

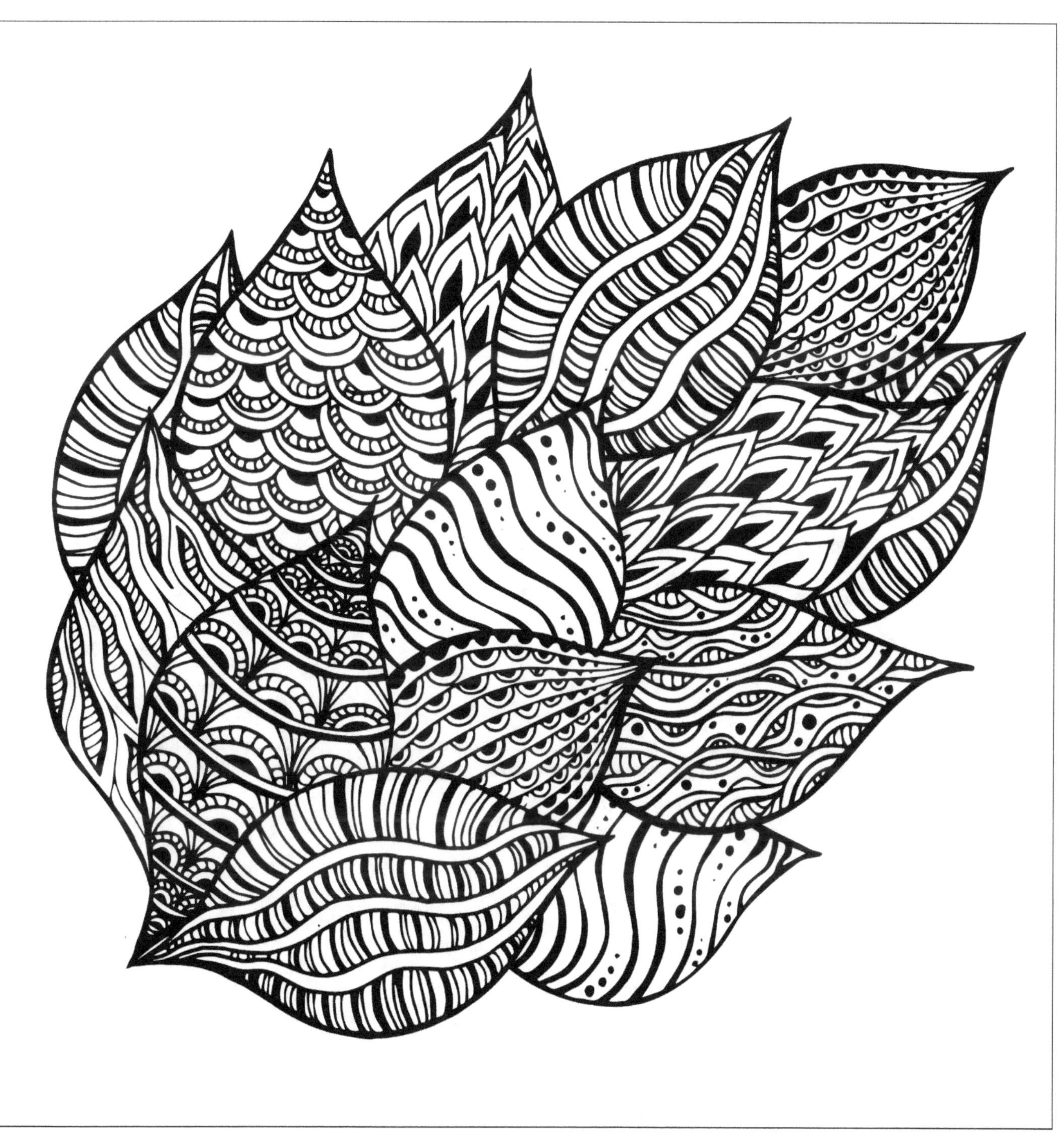

Revelation unites you directly with God.
Miracles unite you directly with your brother.

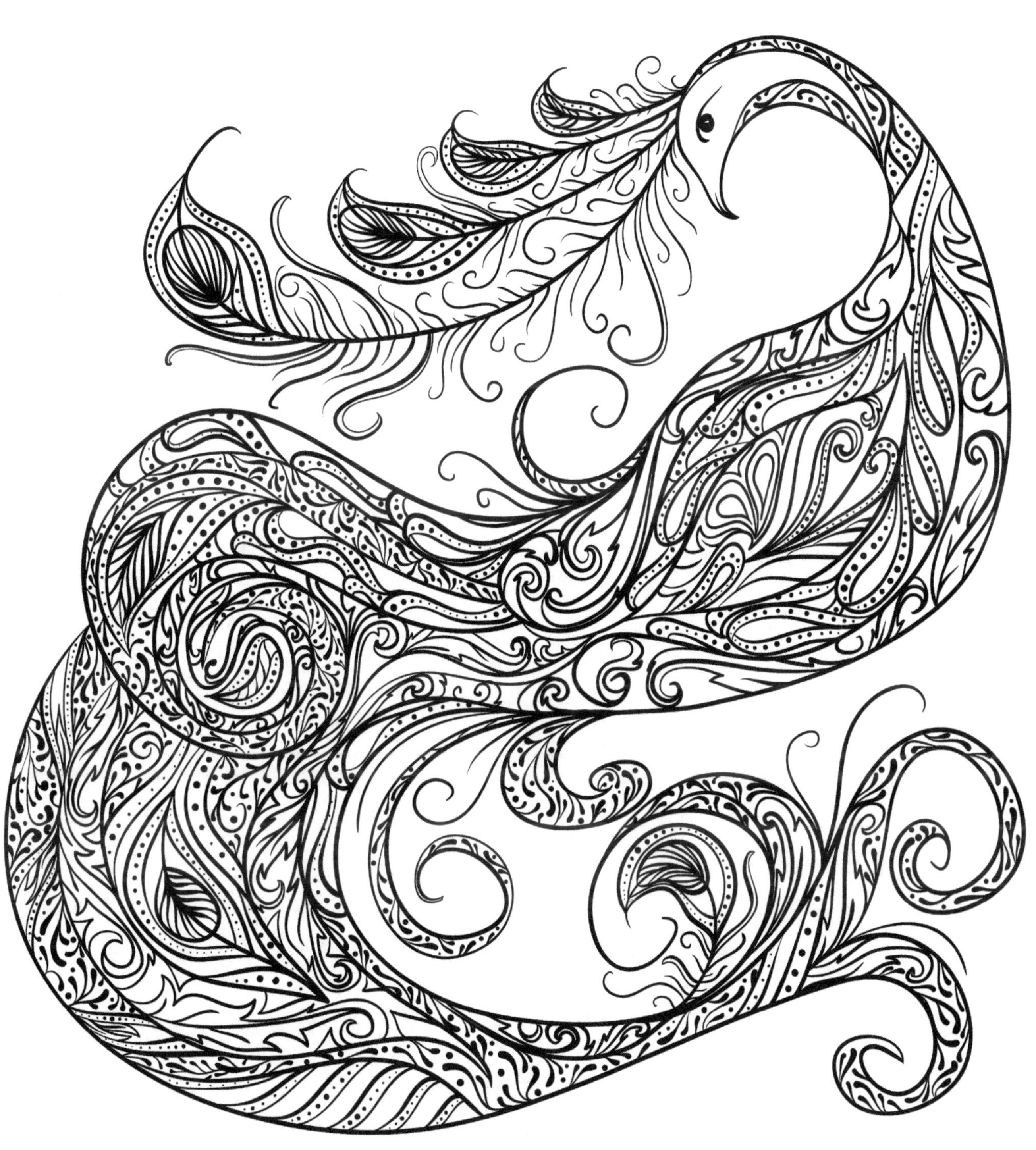

To perceive the healing of your brother as the healing of yourself
is thus the way to remember God.

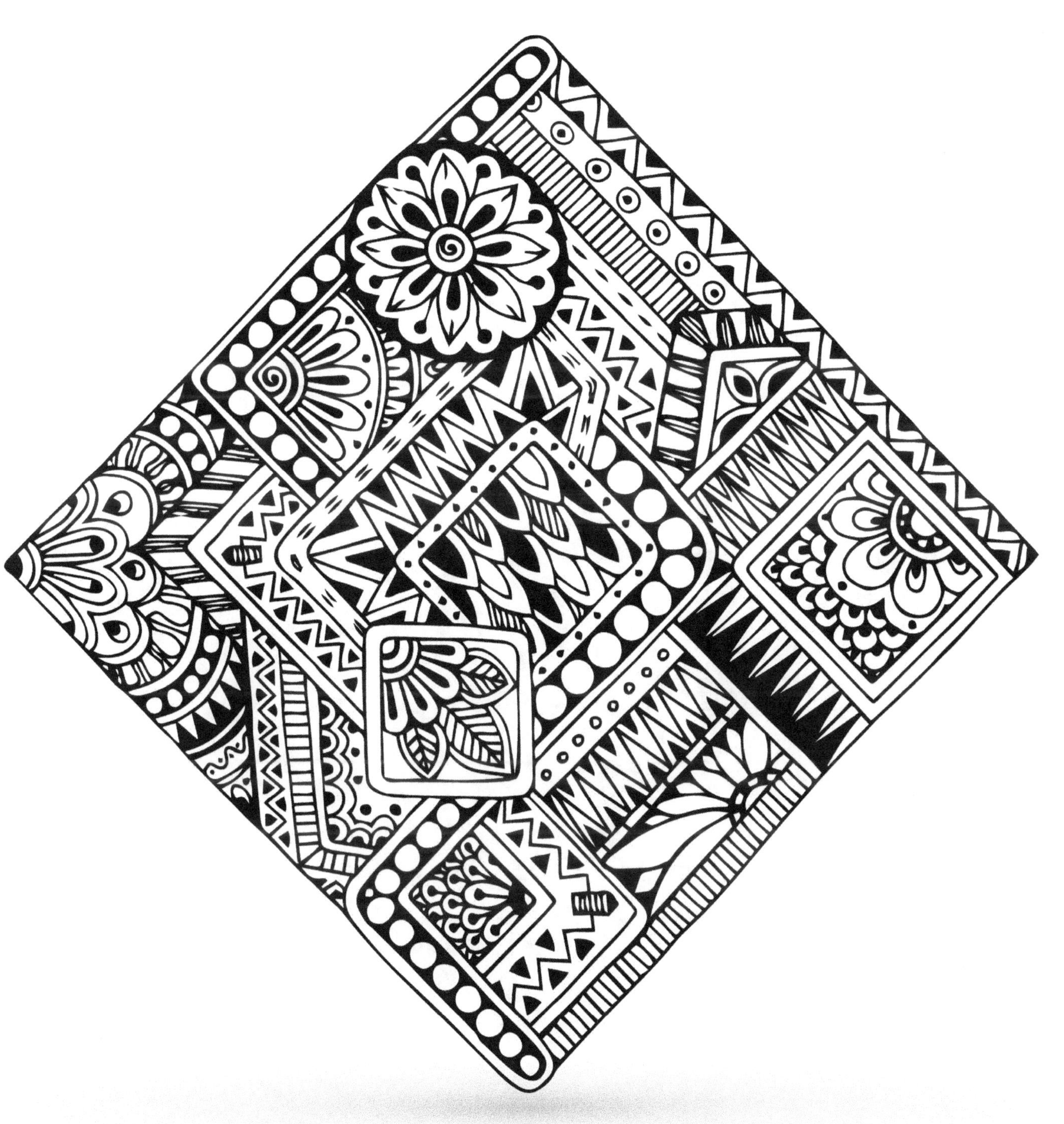

All healing is essentially the release from fear.

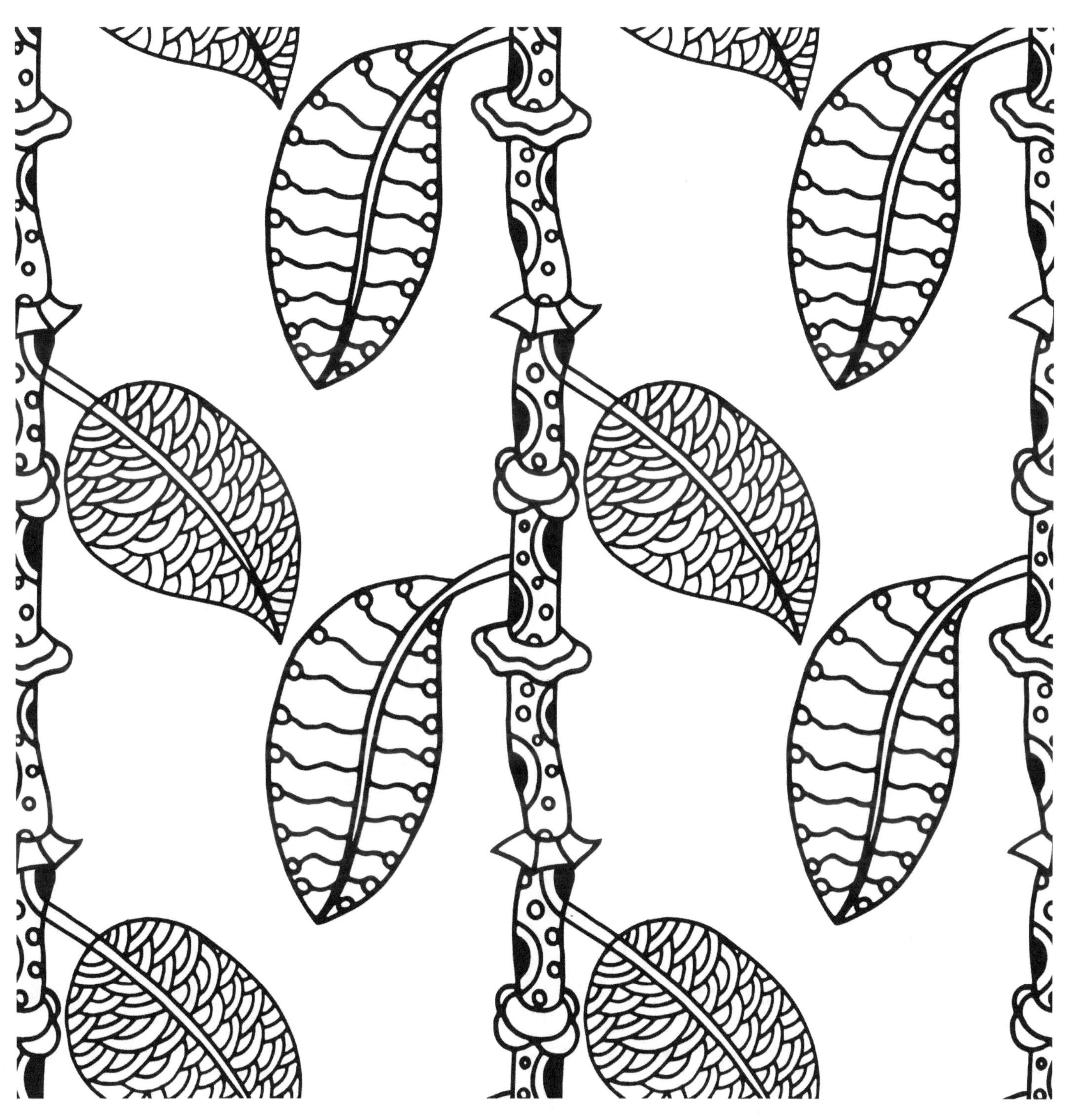

You cannot behold the world and know God.
Only one is true.

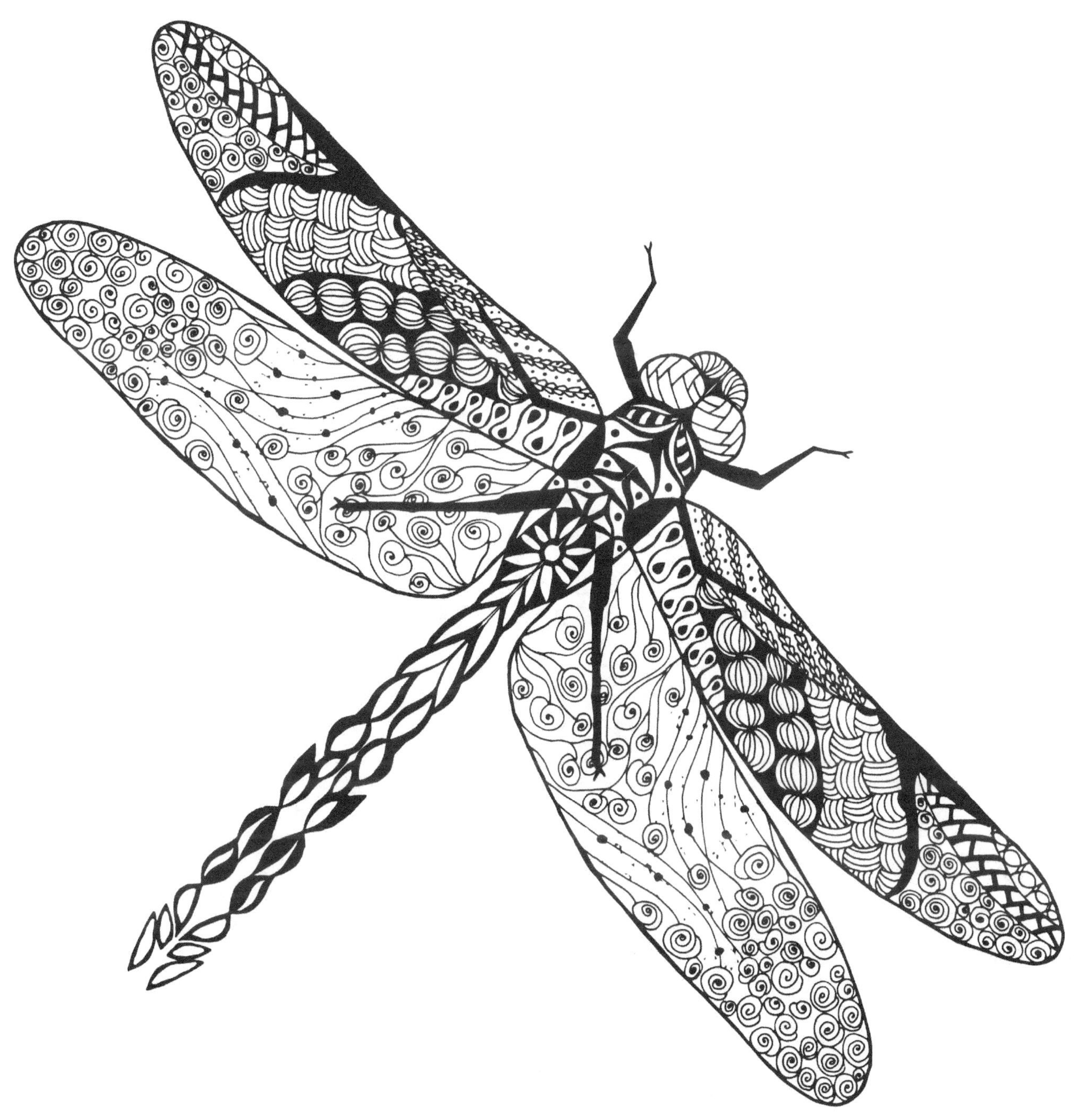

The only meaningful prayer is for forgiveness,
because those who have been forgiven have everything.

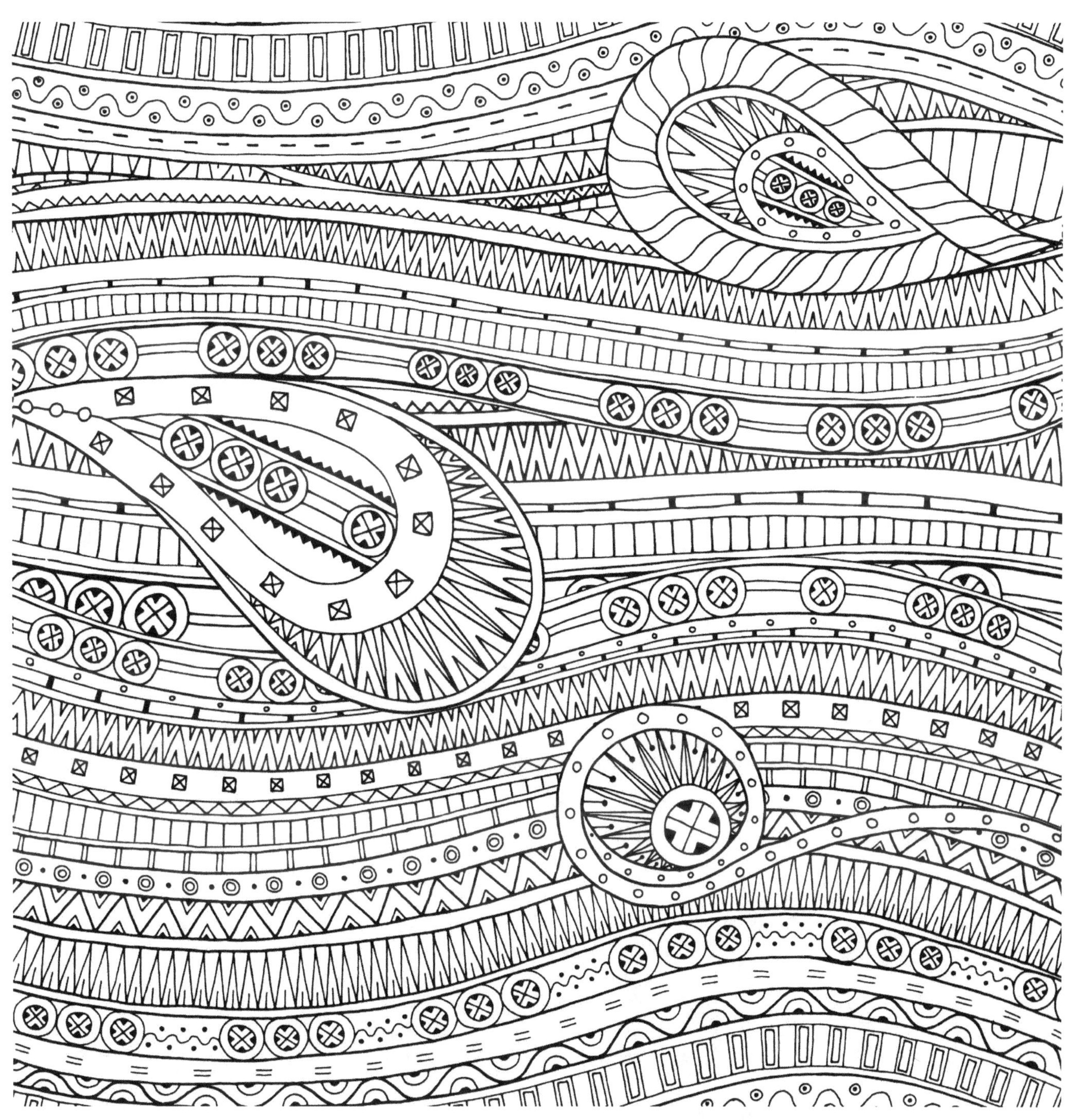

Remember that forgiveness is not loss,
but your salvation.

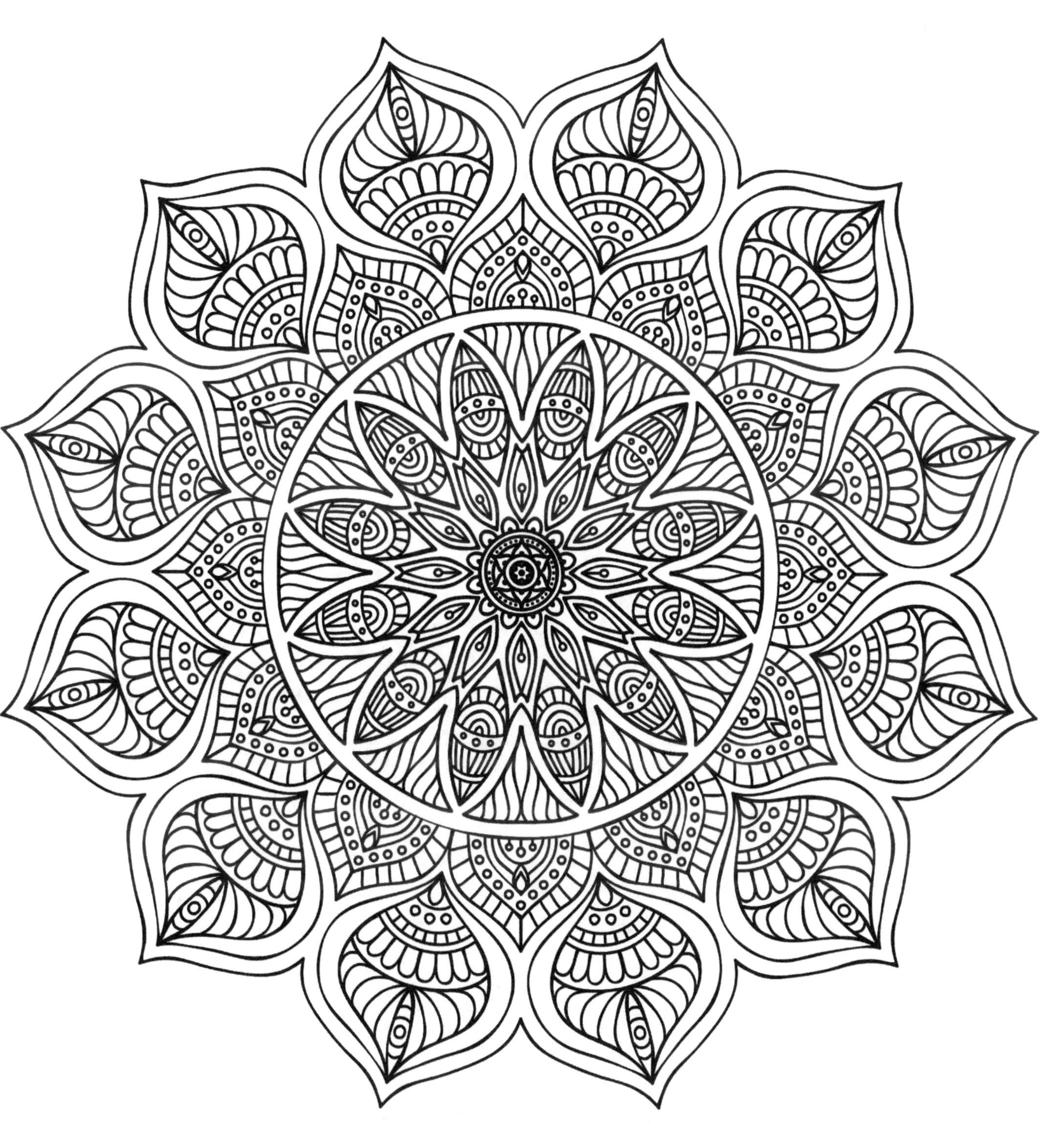

You who want peace can only find it by complete forgiveness.

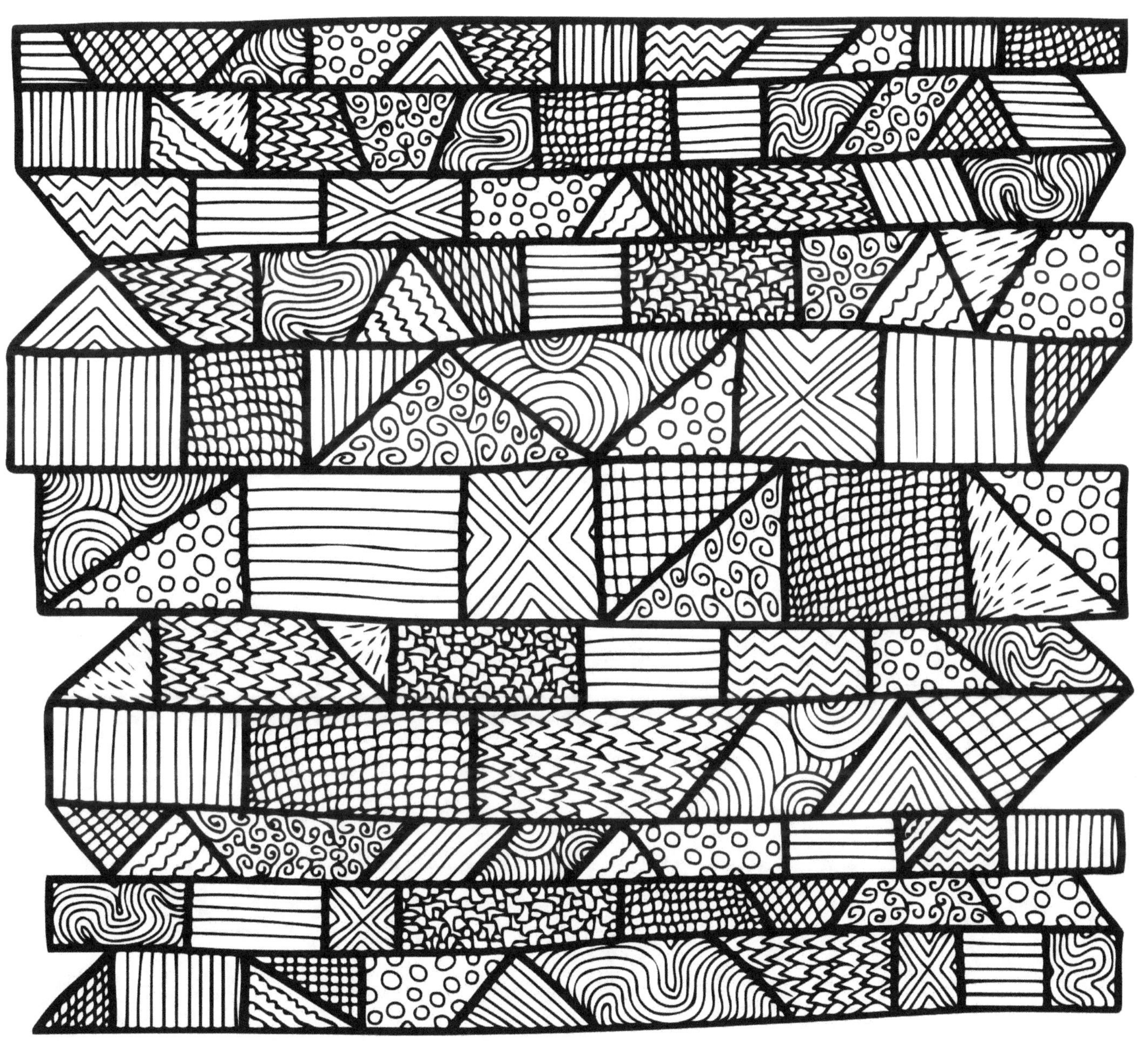

Our task is not to seek for love. It is to seek for all of the barriers that we have built that stand in the way.

It has taken time to misguide you so completely,
but it takes no time at all to be what you are.

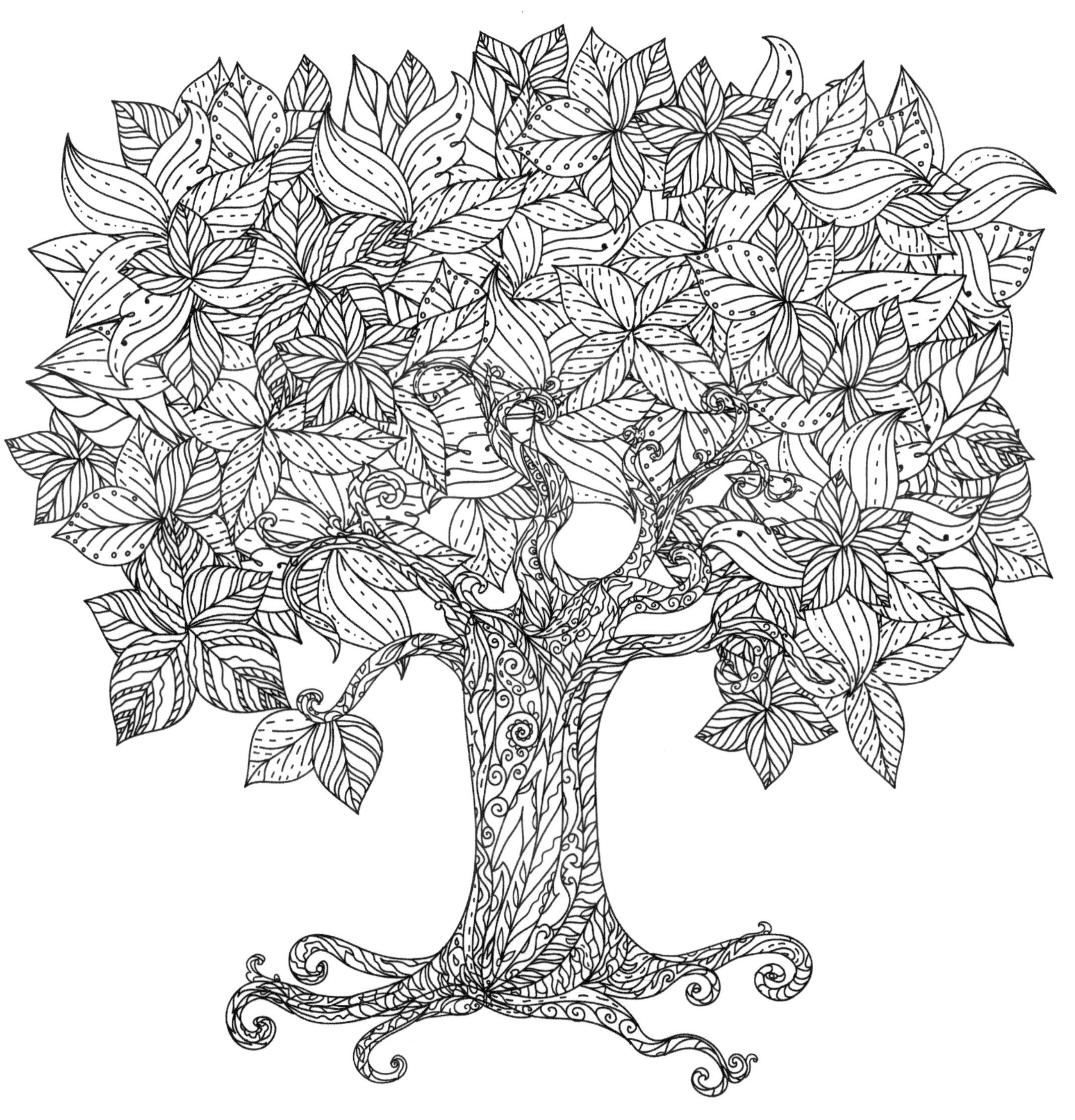

Take this very instant, now, and think of it
as all there is of time.

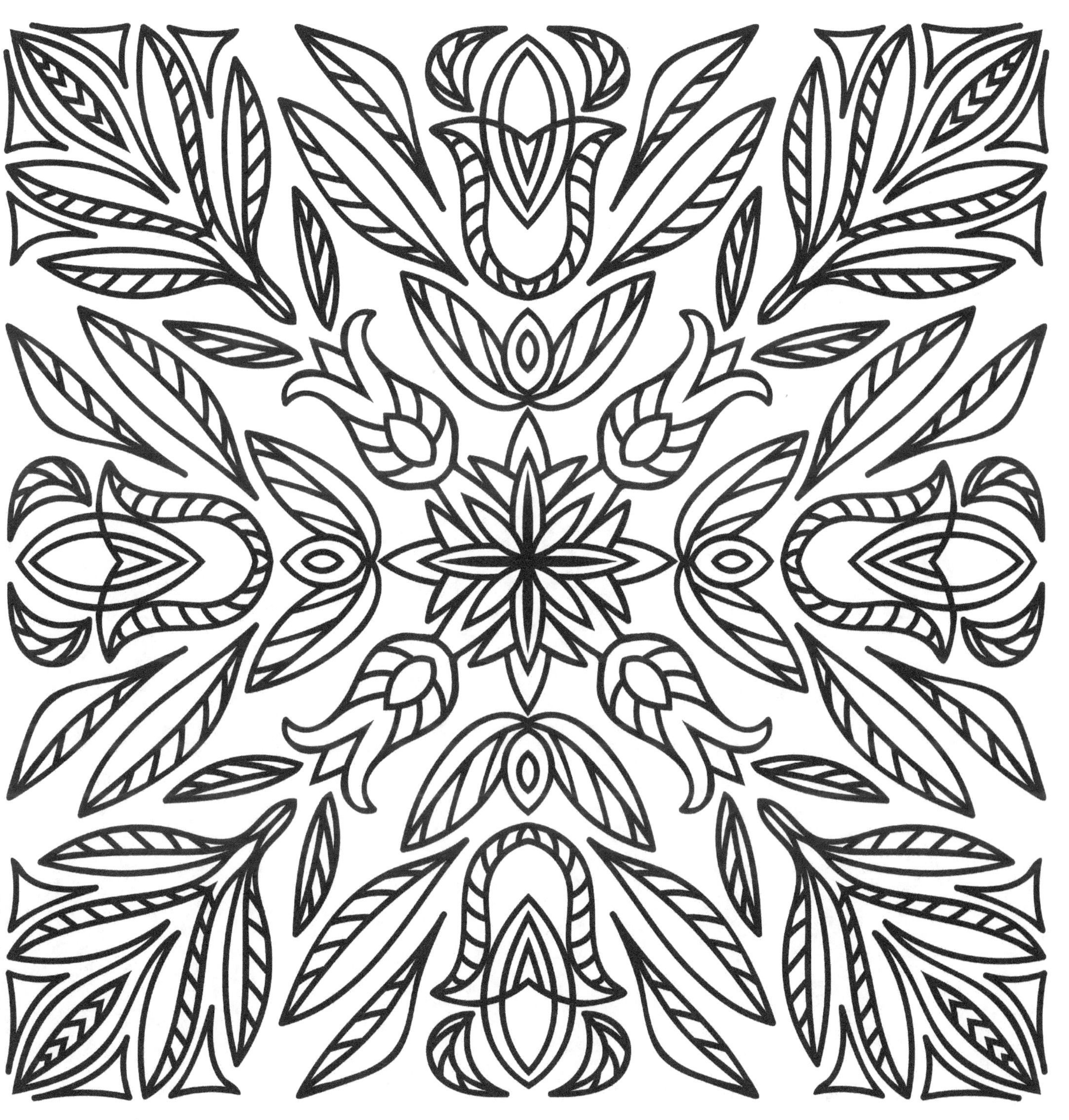

To learn to separate out this single second, and to experience it as timeless, is to begin to experience yourself as not separate.

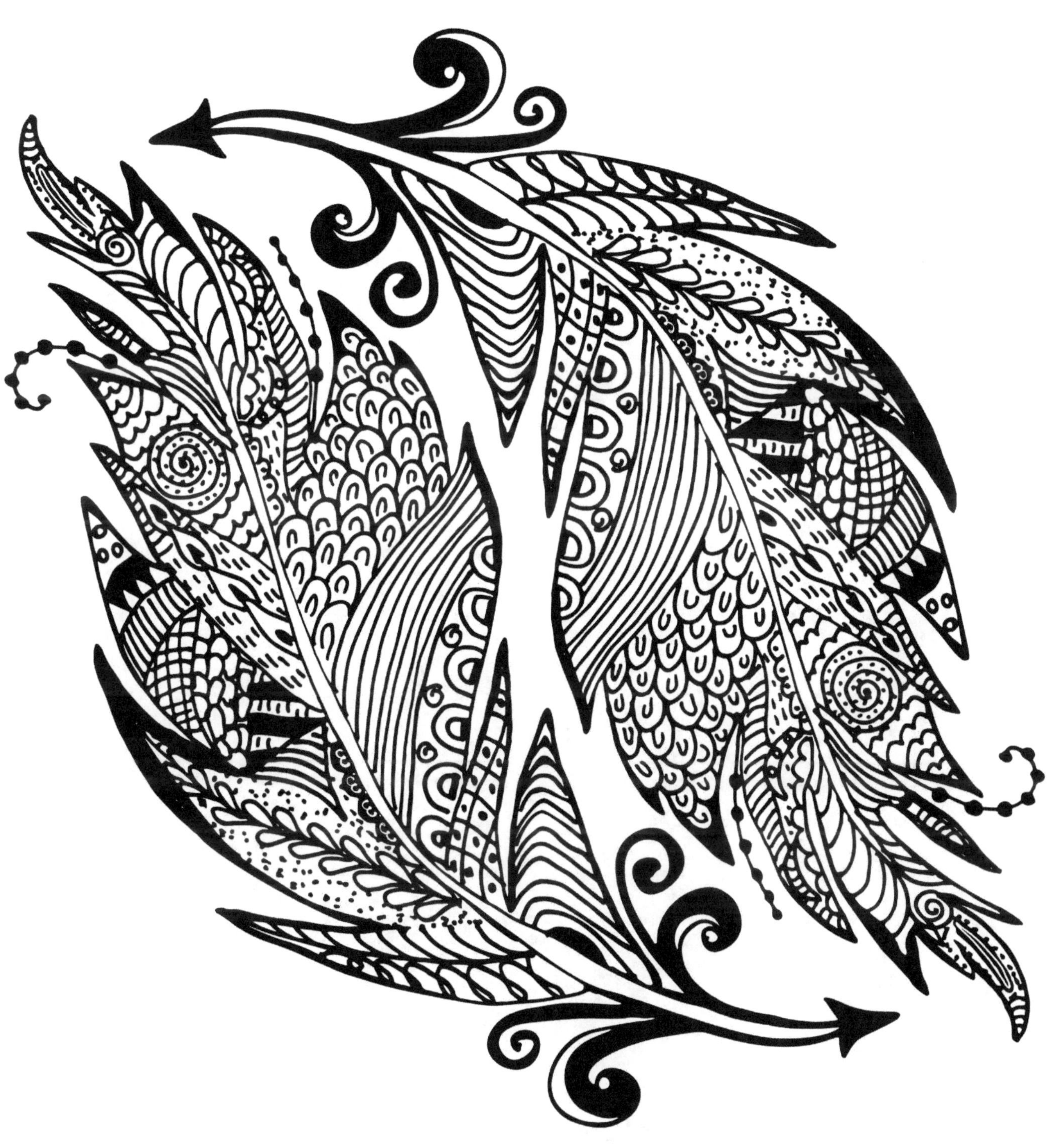

Heaven is here. There is nowhere else.
Heaven is now. There is no other time.

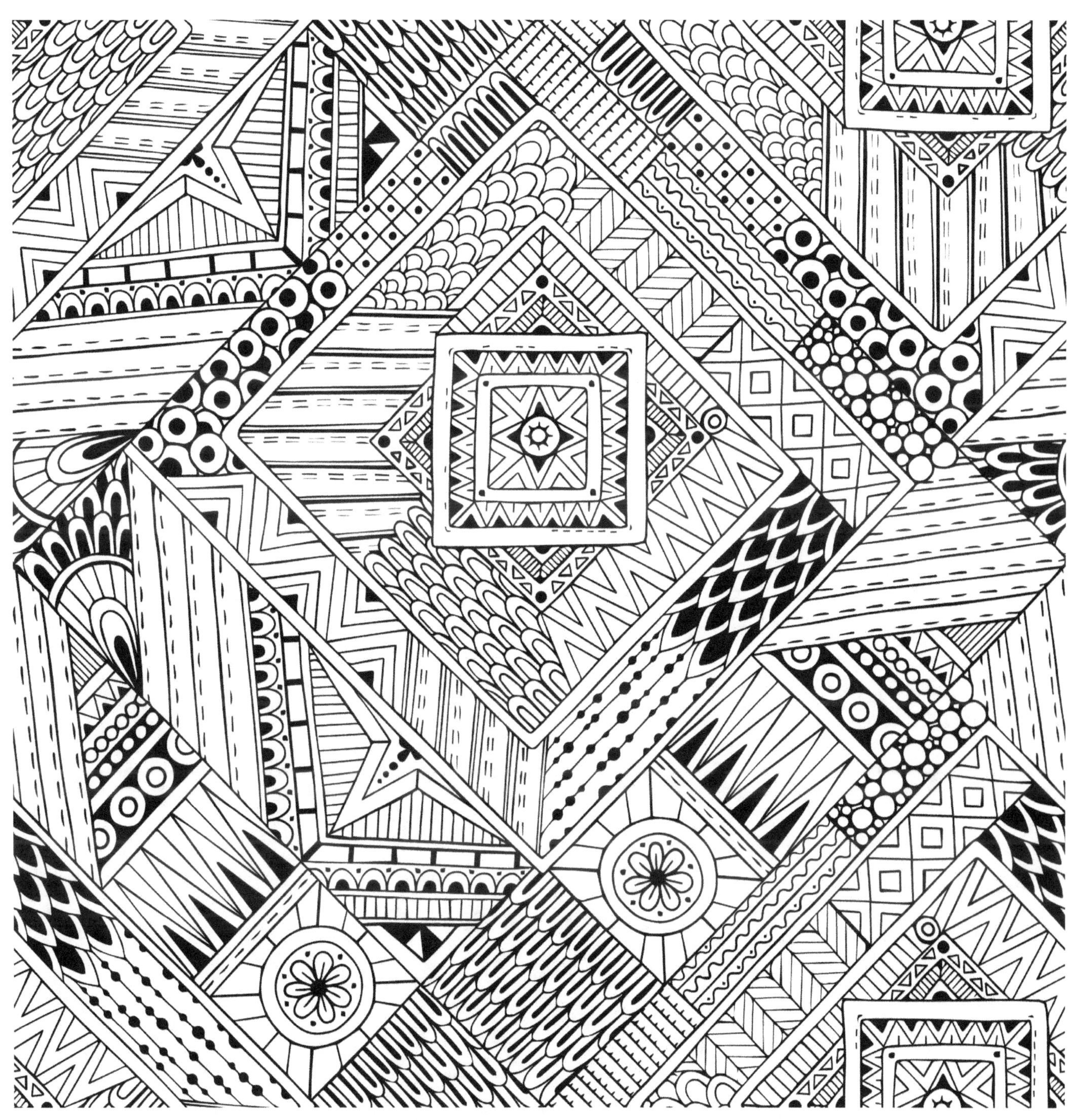

Hold onto nothing. Do not bring with you one thought the past has taught, nor one belief you ever learned before from anything.

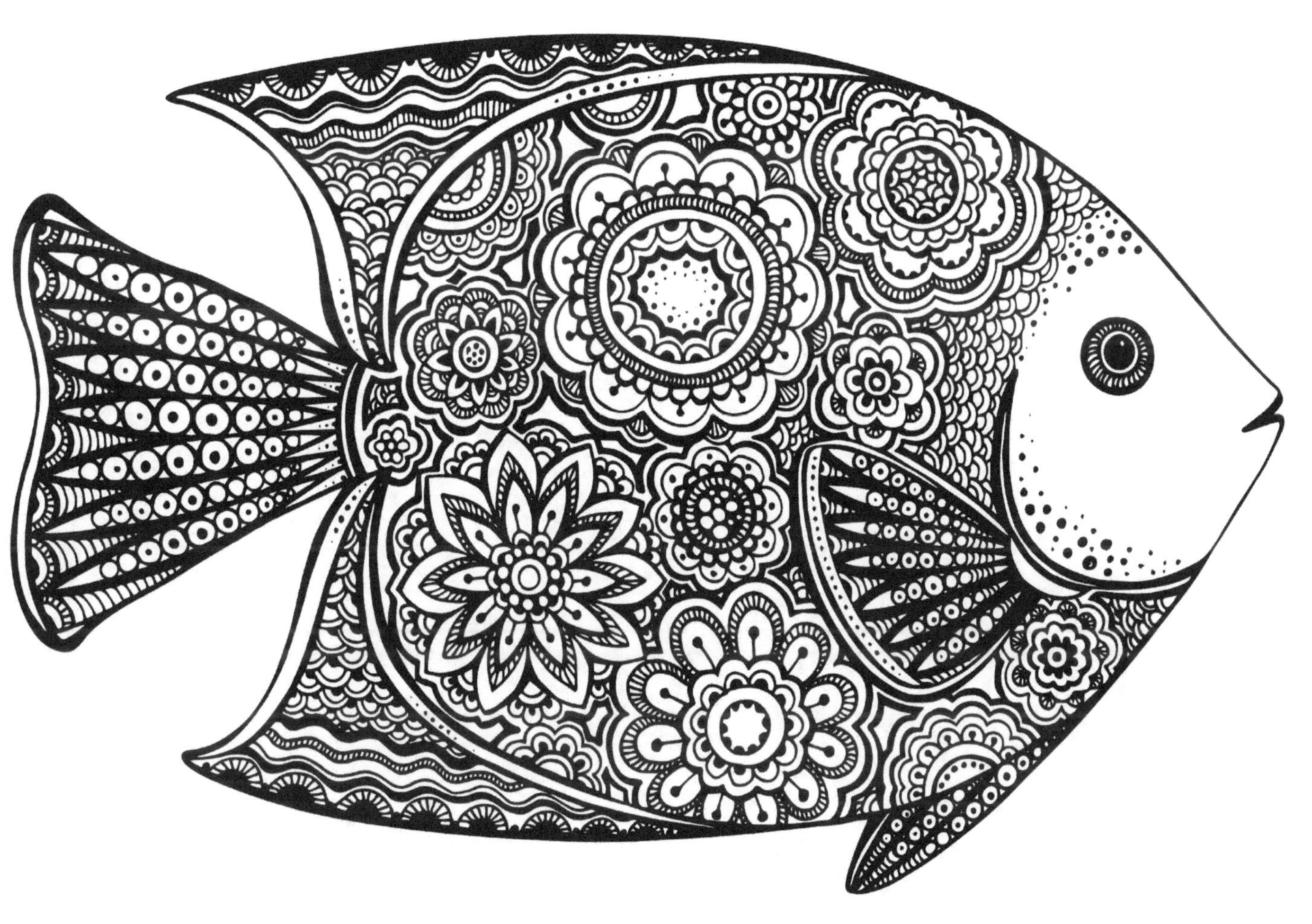

Time is inconceivable without change,
yet holiness does not change.

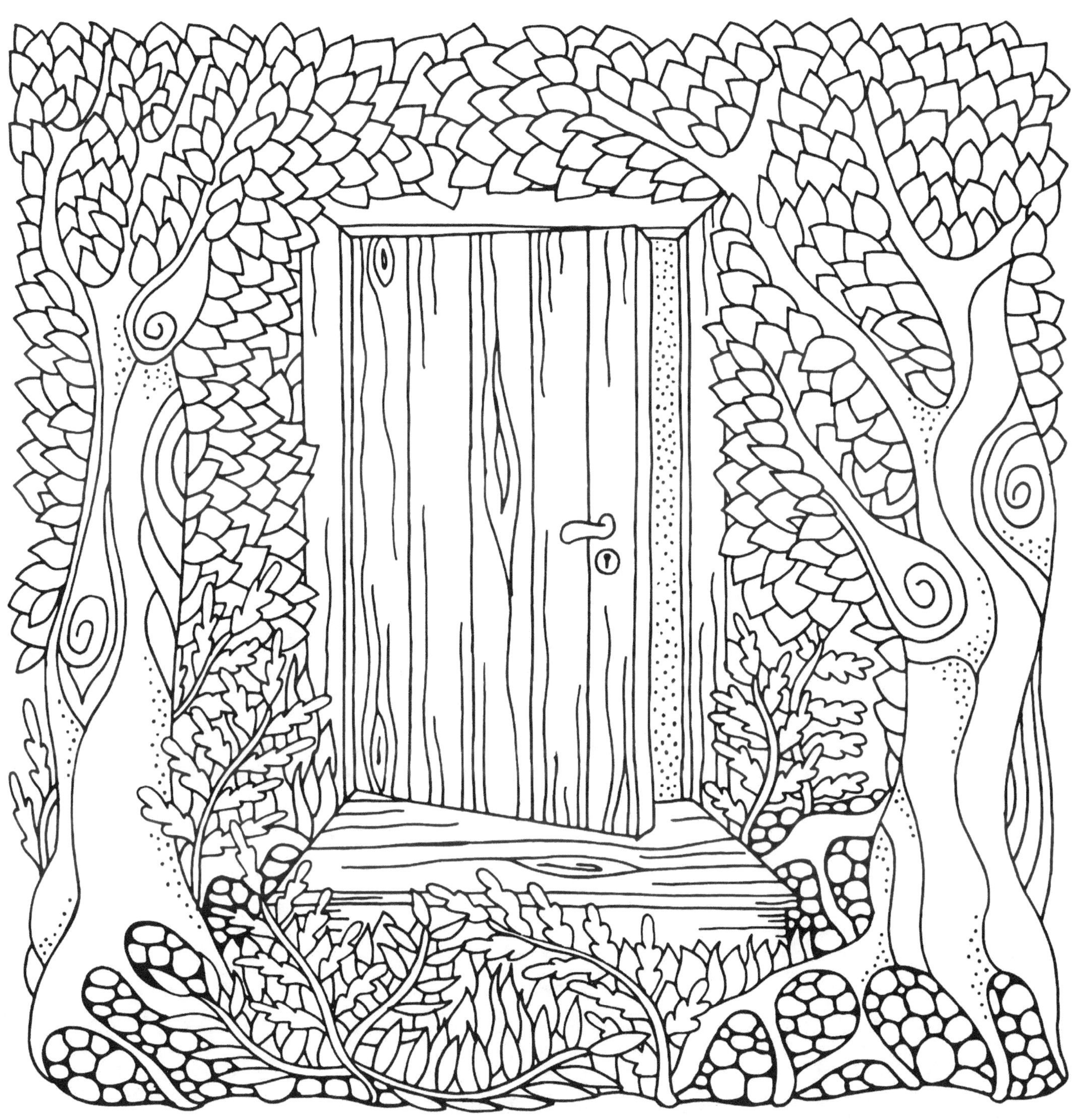

He Who transcends time for you understands what time is for. Holiness lies not in time, but in eternity.

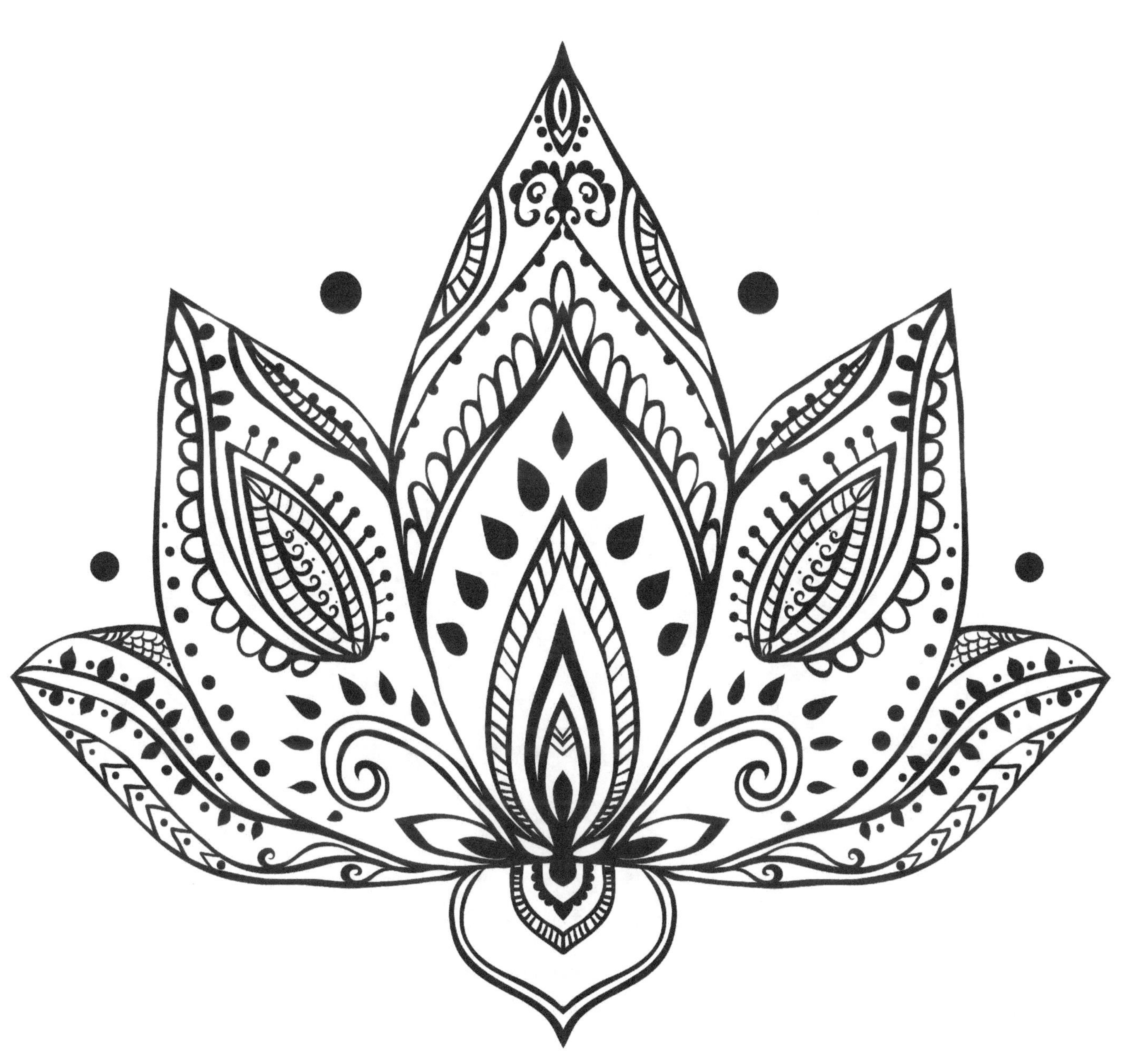

What holds remembrance of God cannot be bound by time.
No more are you.

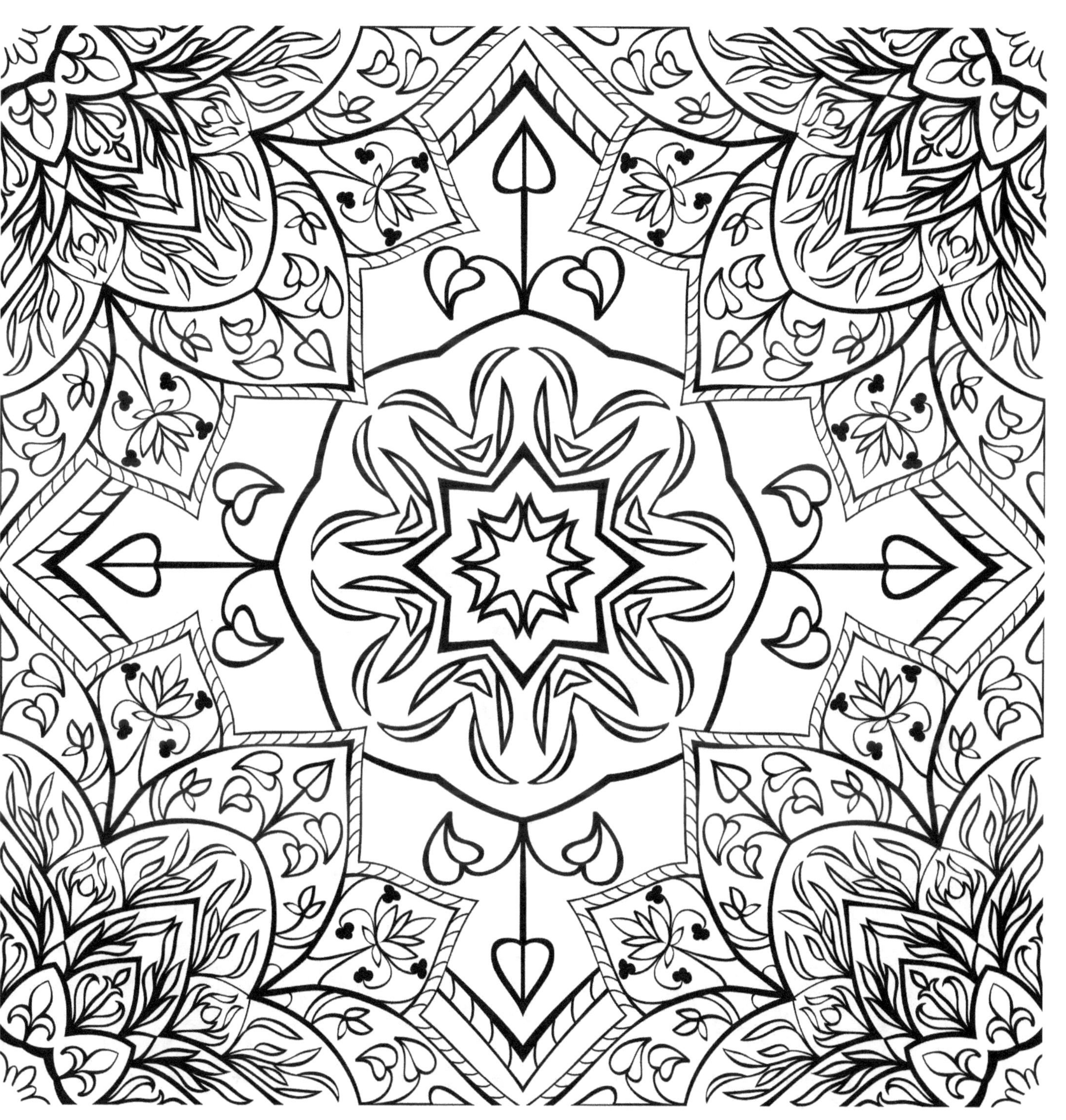

Truth is so far beyond time that all of it happens at once.
For as it was created one, so its oneness depends not on time at all.

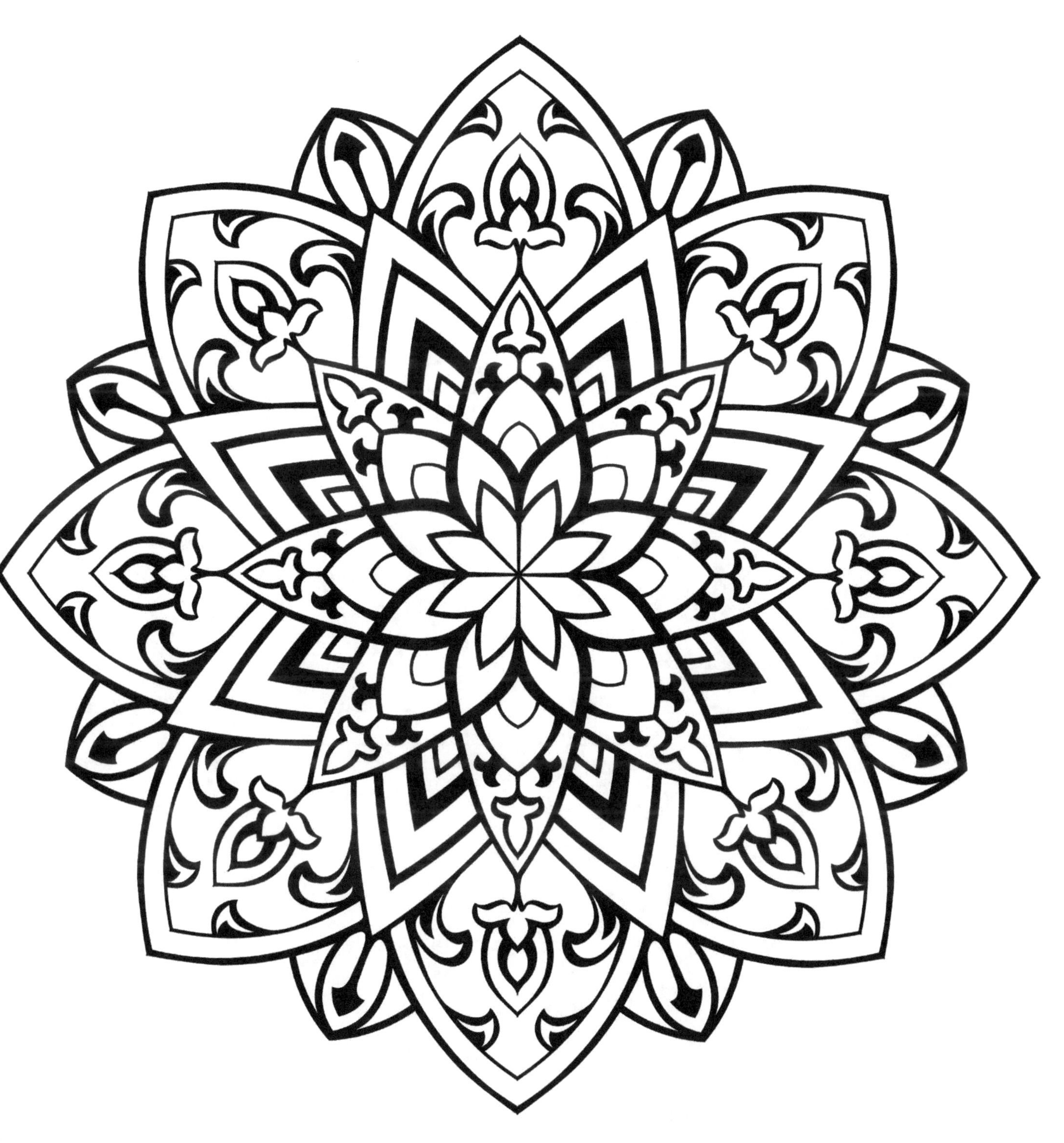

You are the work of God, and His work is wholly lovable and wholly loving.

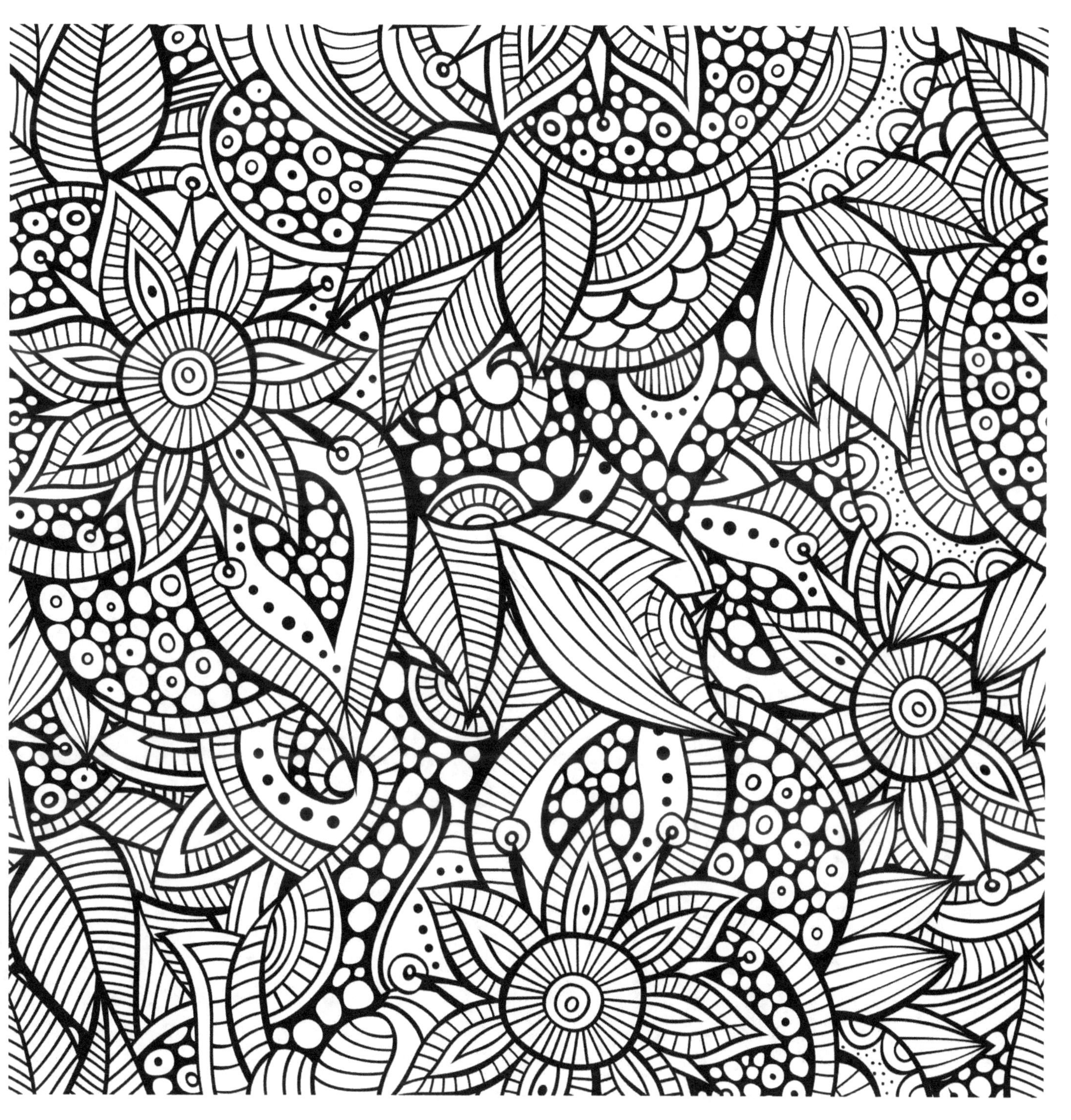

God is incomplete without you because His grandeur is total,
and you cannot be missing from it.

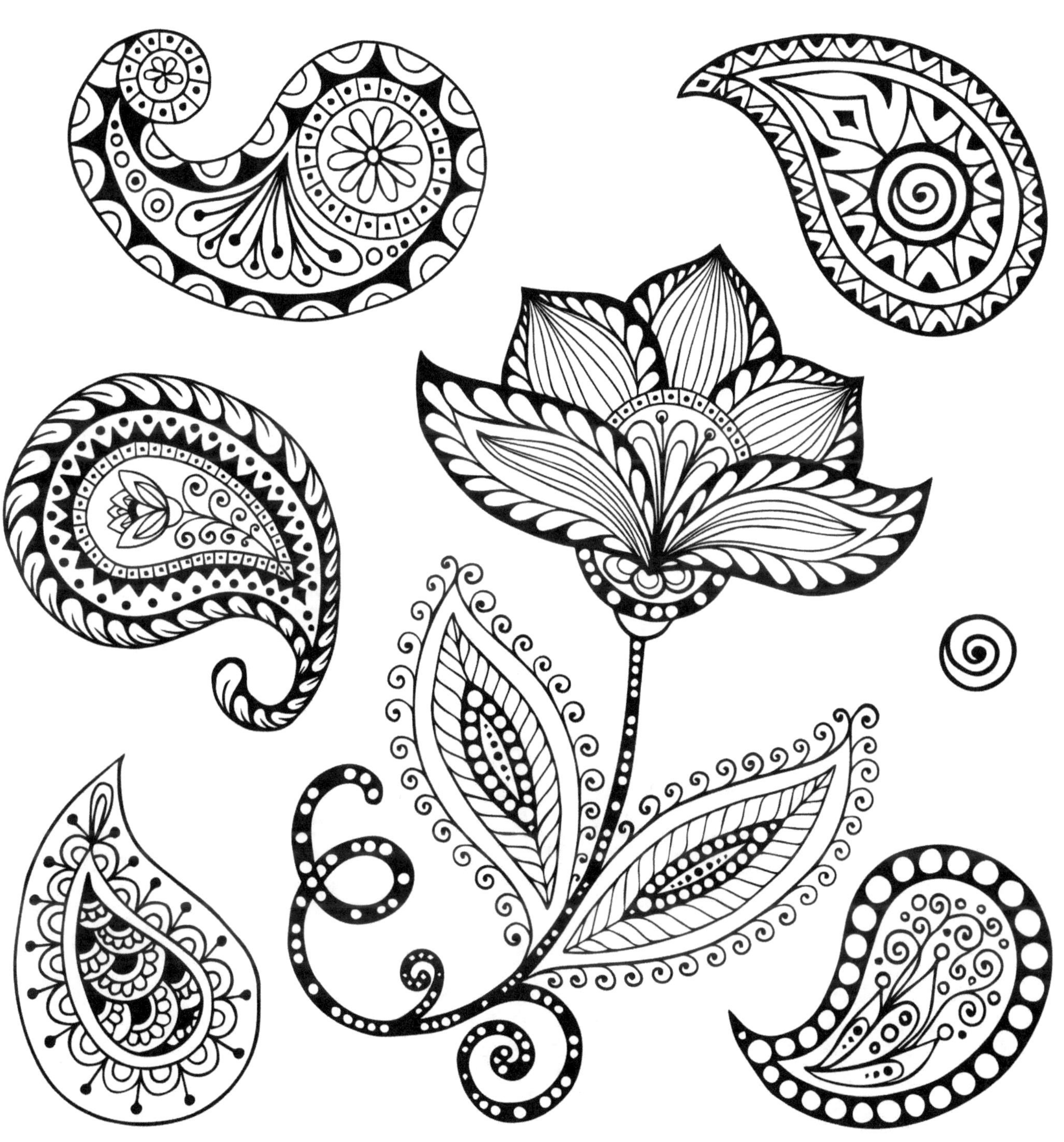

Whatever is true is eternal, and cannot change or be changed.

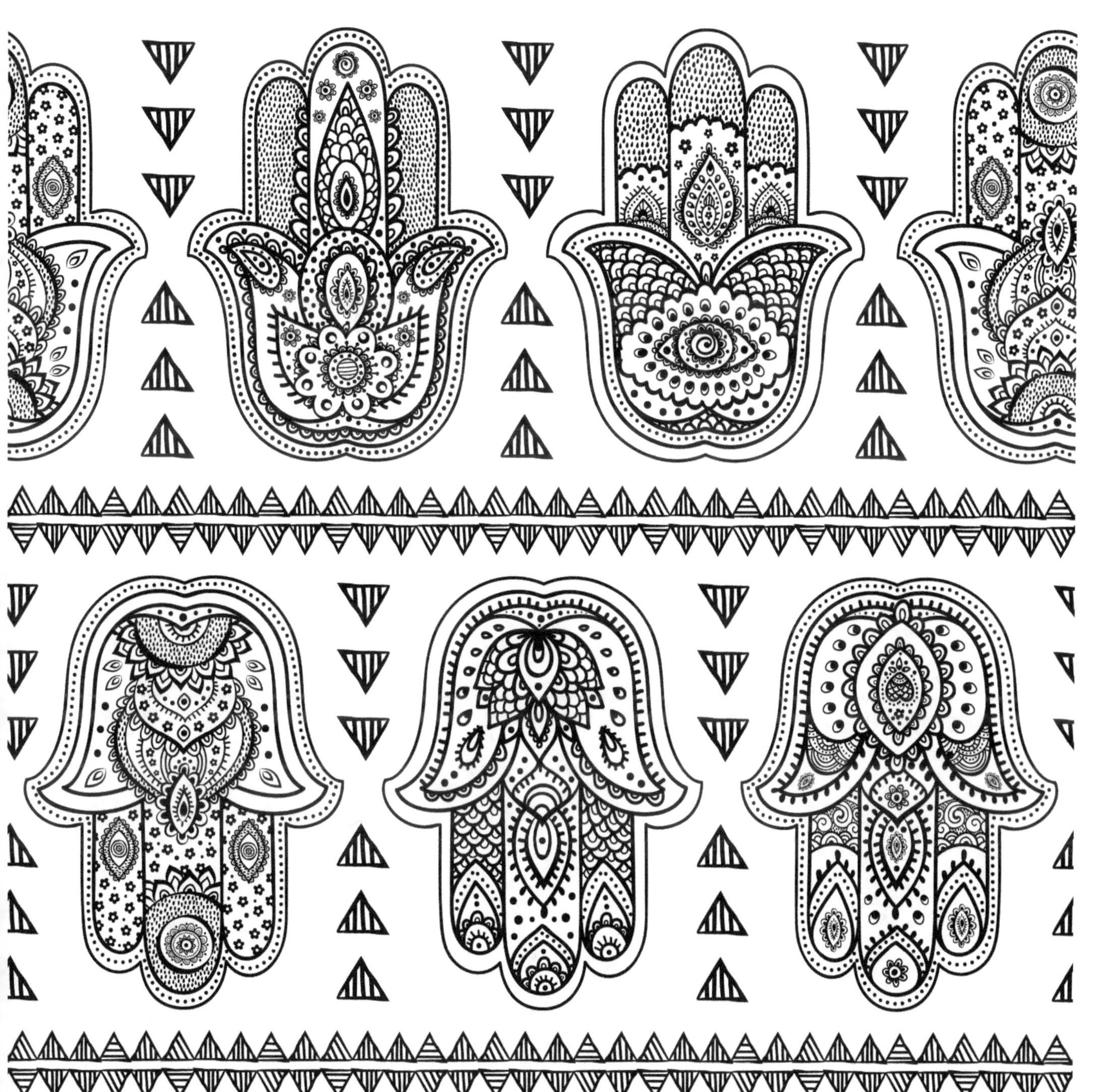

Remember that You did not create yourself.

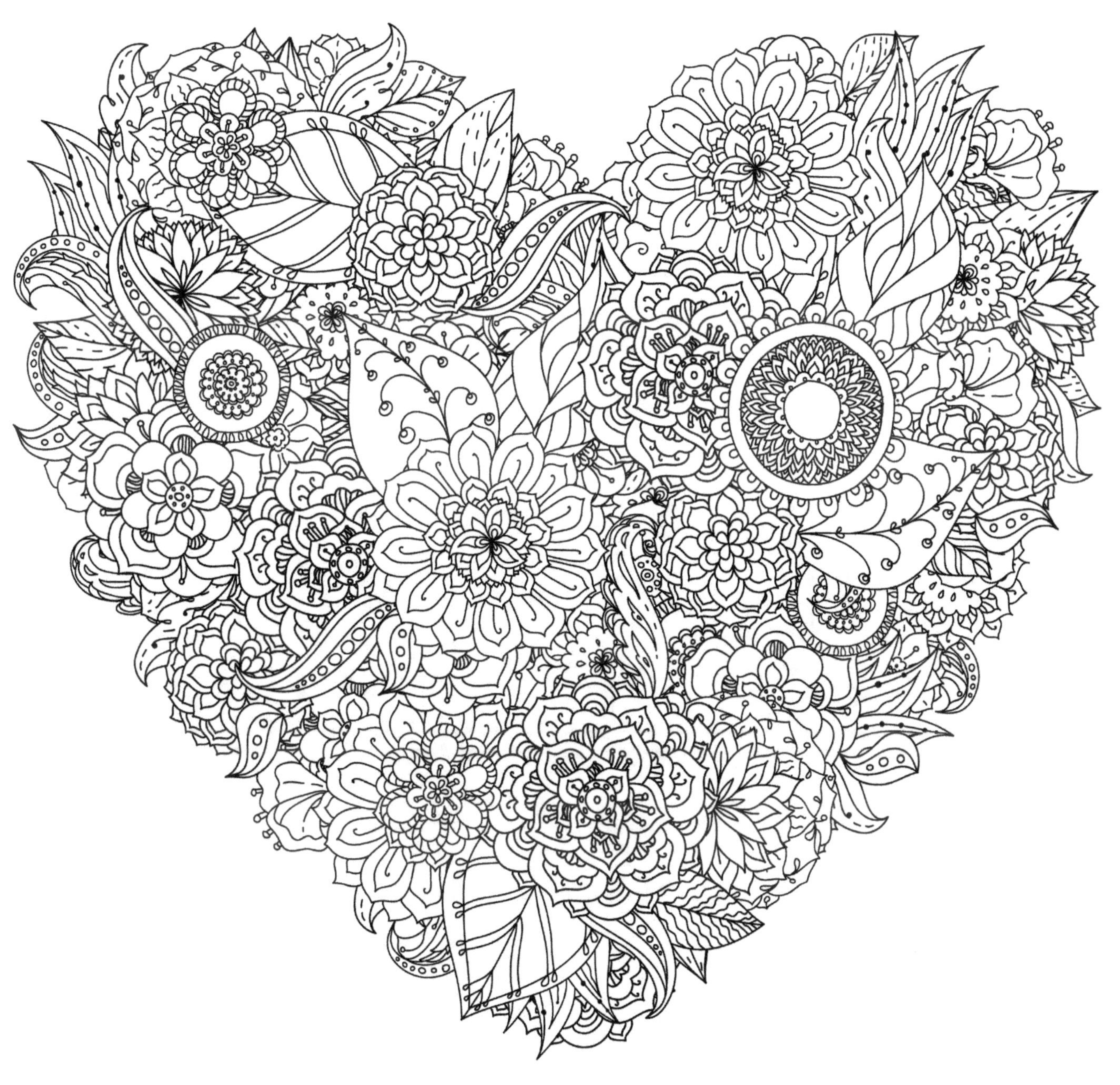

You cannot behold the world and know God. Only one is true.

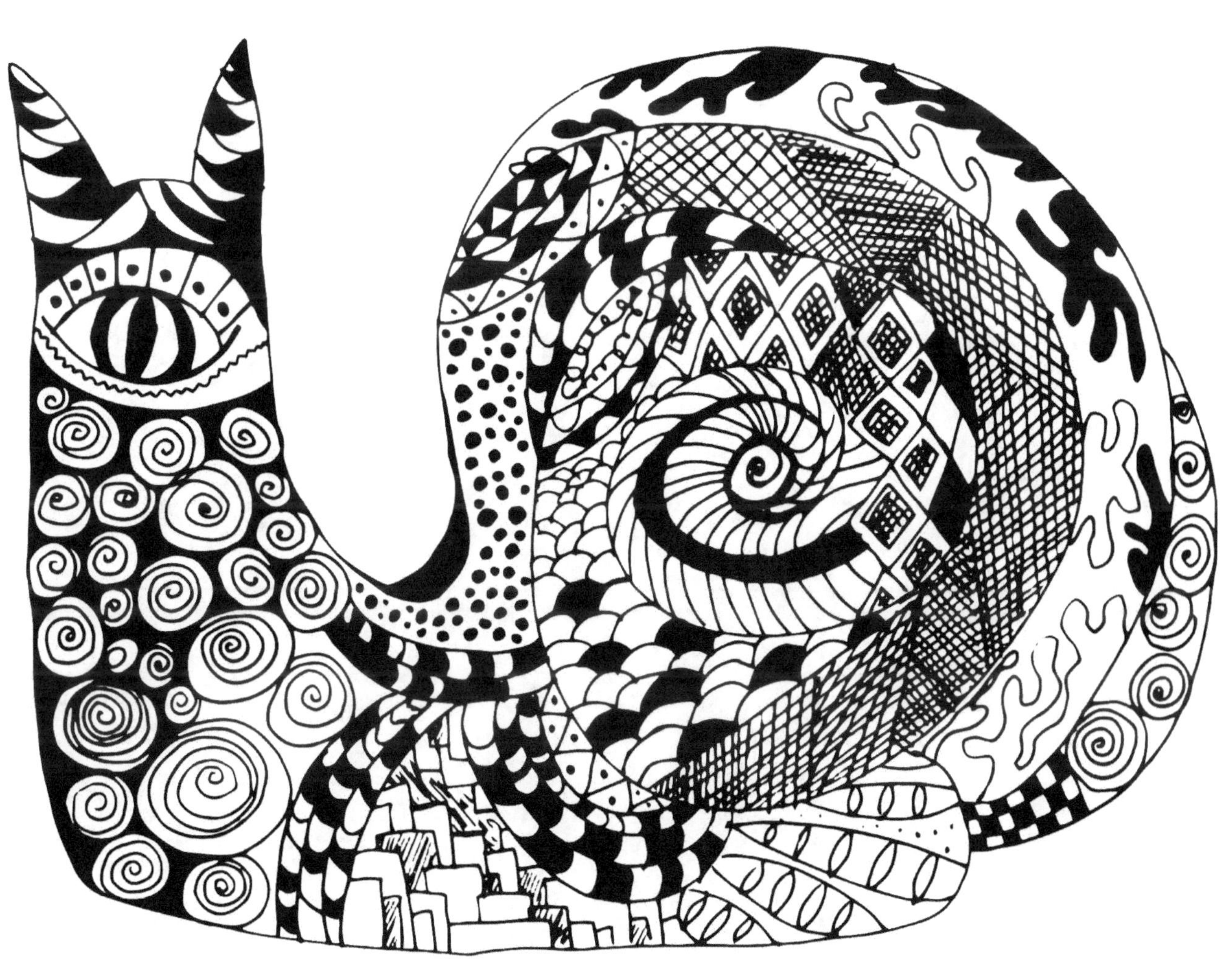

It is only in Heaven that God would have you be.

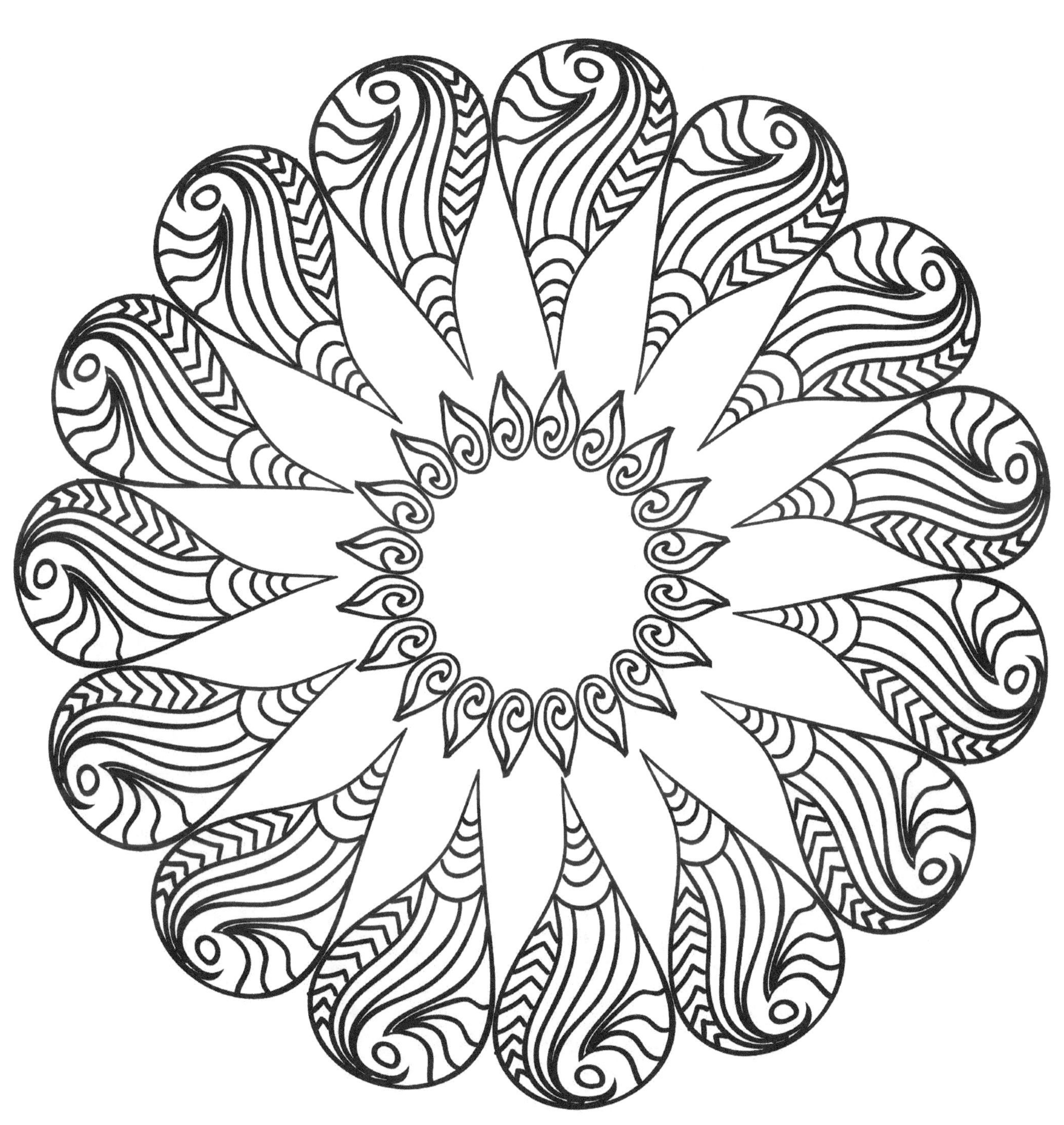

Spirit is in a state of grace forever. Your reality is only spirit.
Therefore you are in a state of grace forever.

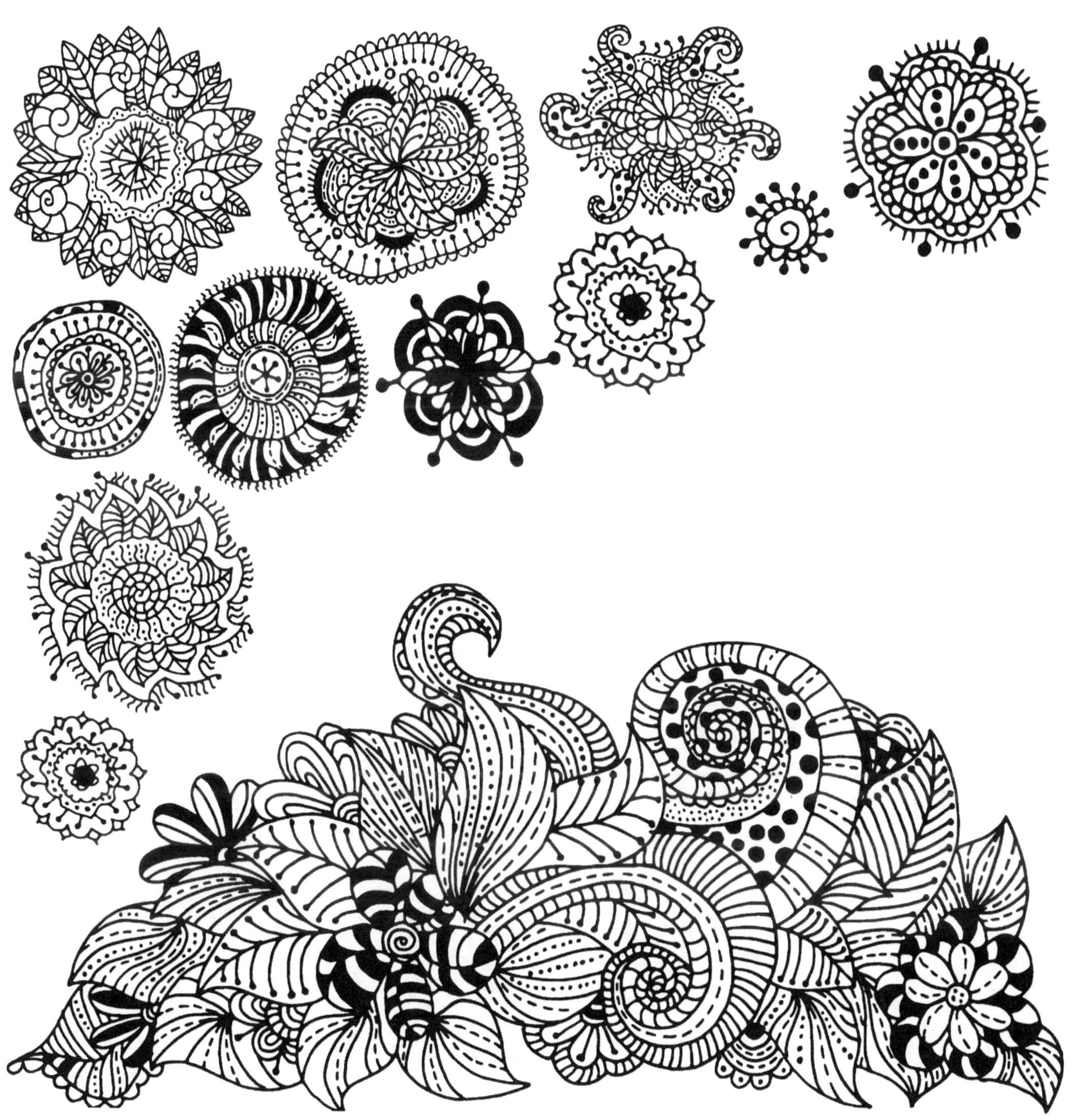

Joy has no cost. It is your sacred right.

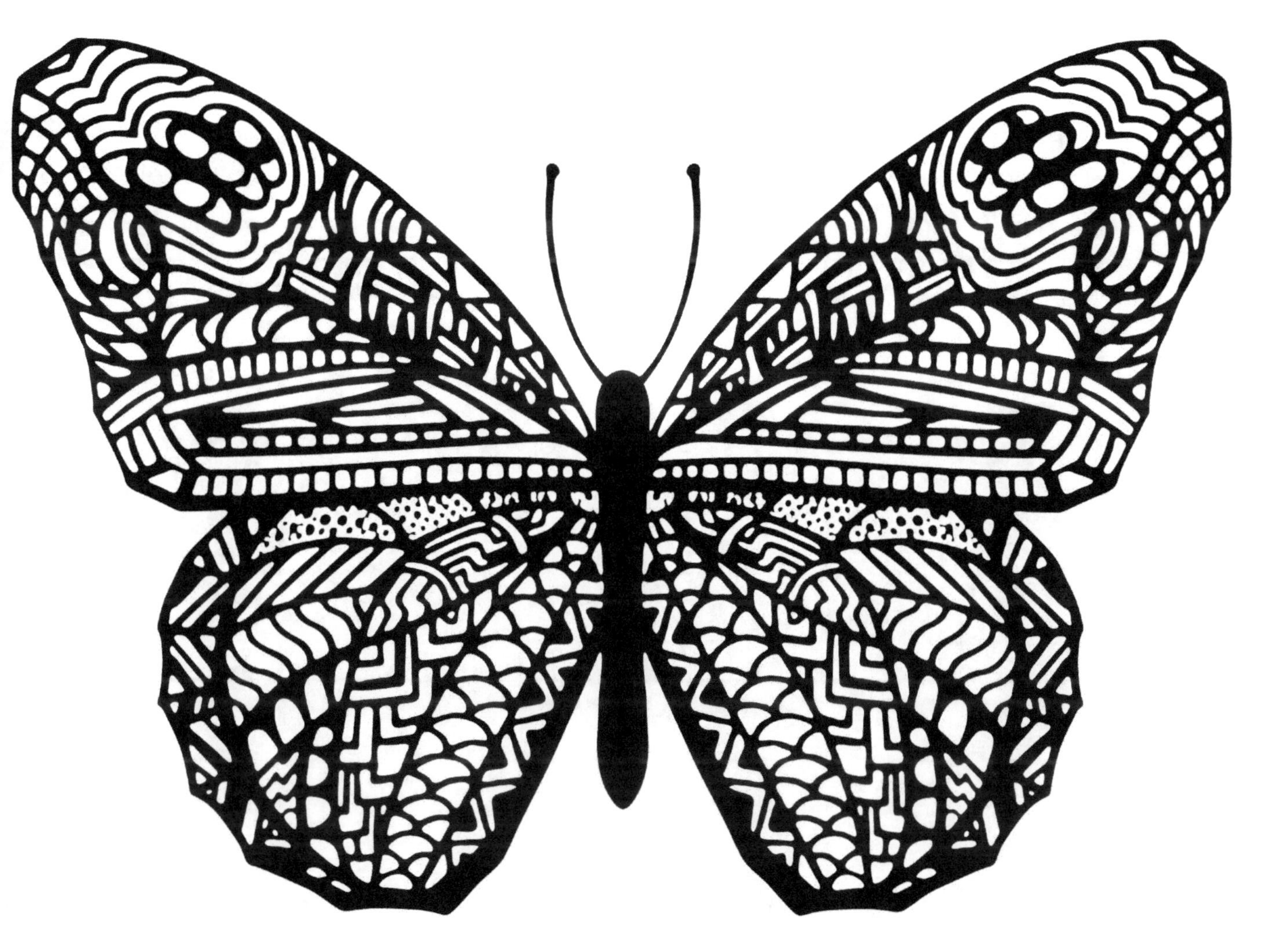

Your ego is never at stake because God did not create it.
Your spirit is never at stake because He did.

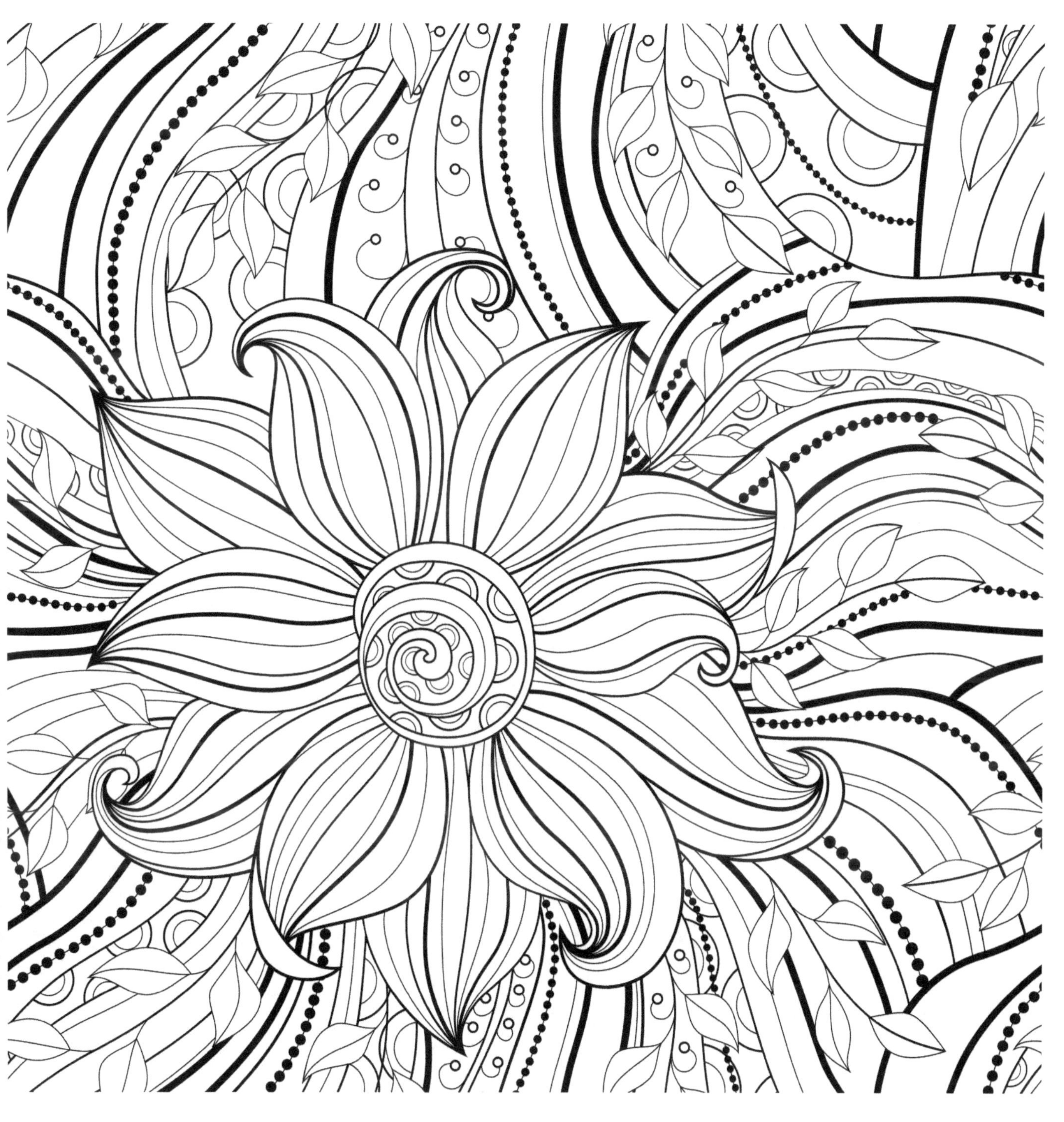

What is not love is always fear, and nothing else.

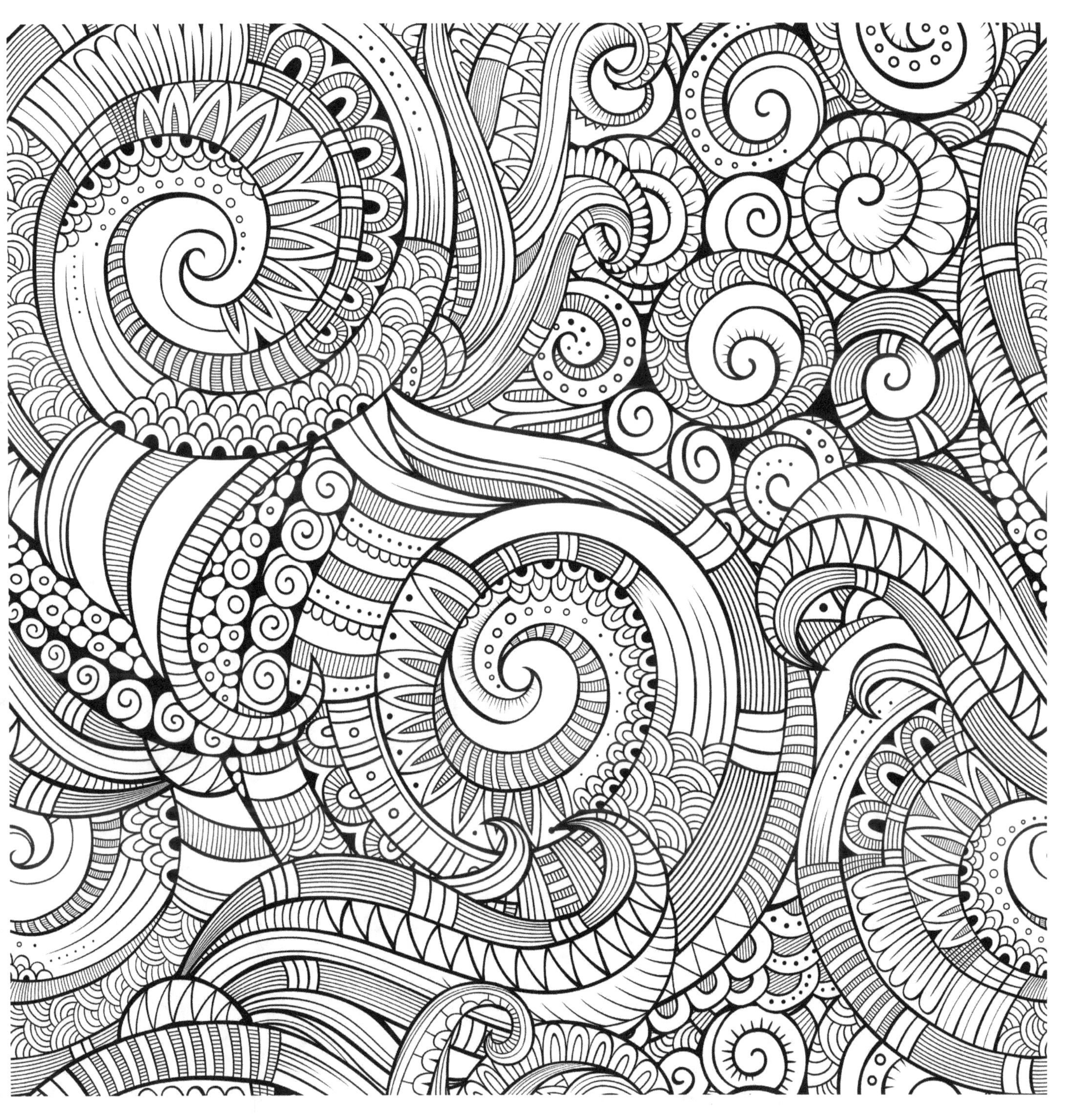

The opposite of love is fear, but what is all-encompassing can have no opposite.

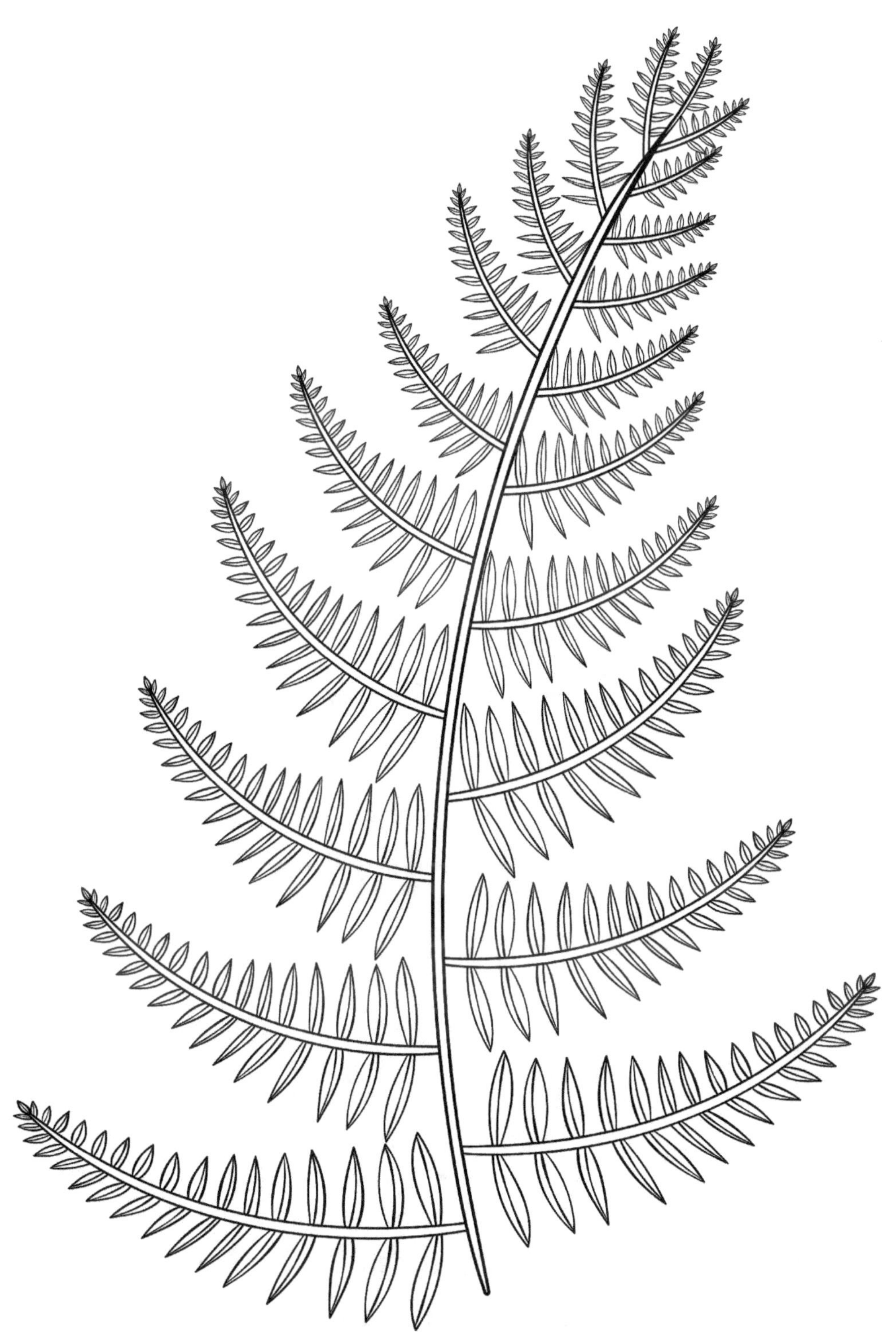

Nothing real can be threatened. Nothing unreal exists.
Herein lies the peace of God.

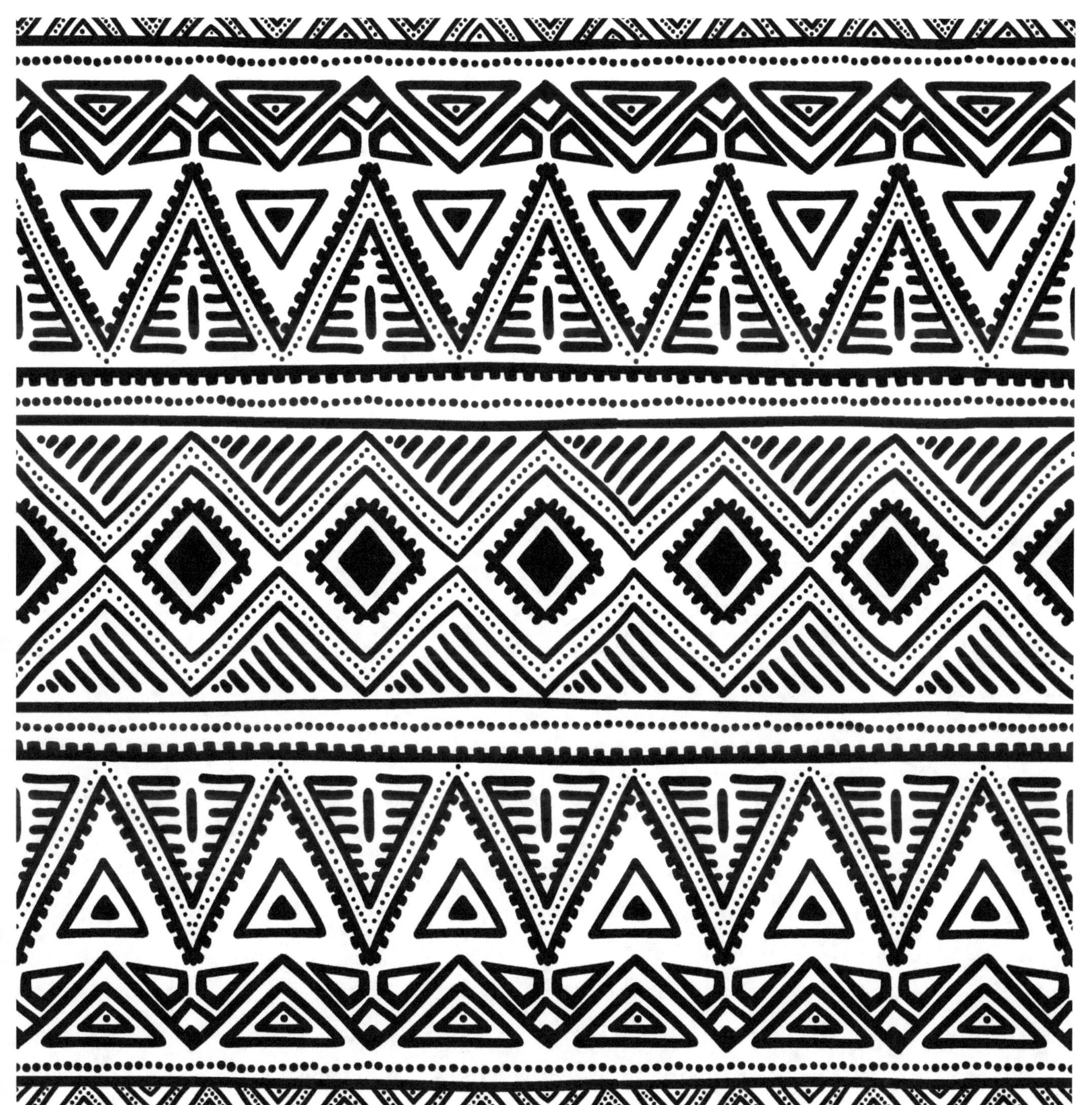

Love is not learned, because there never was a time
in which you knew it not.

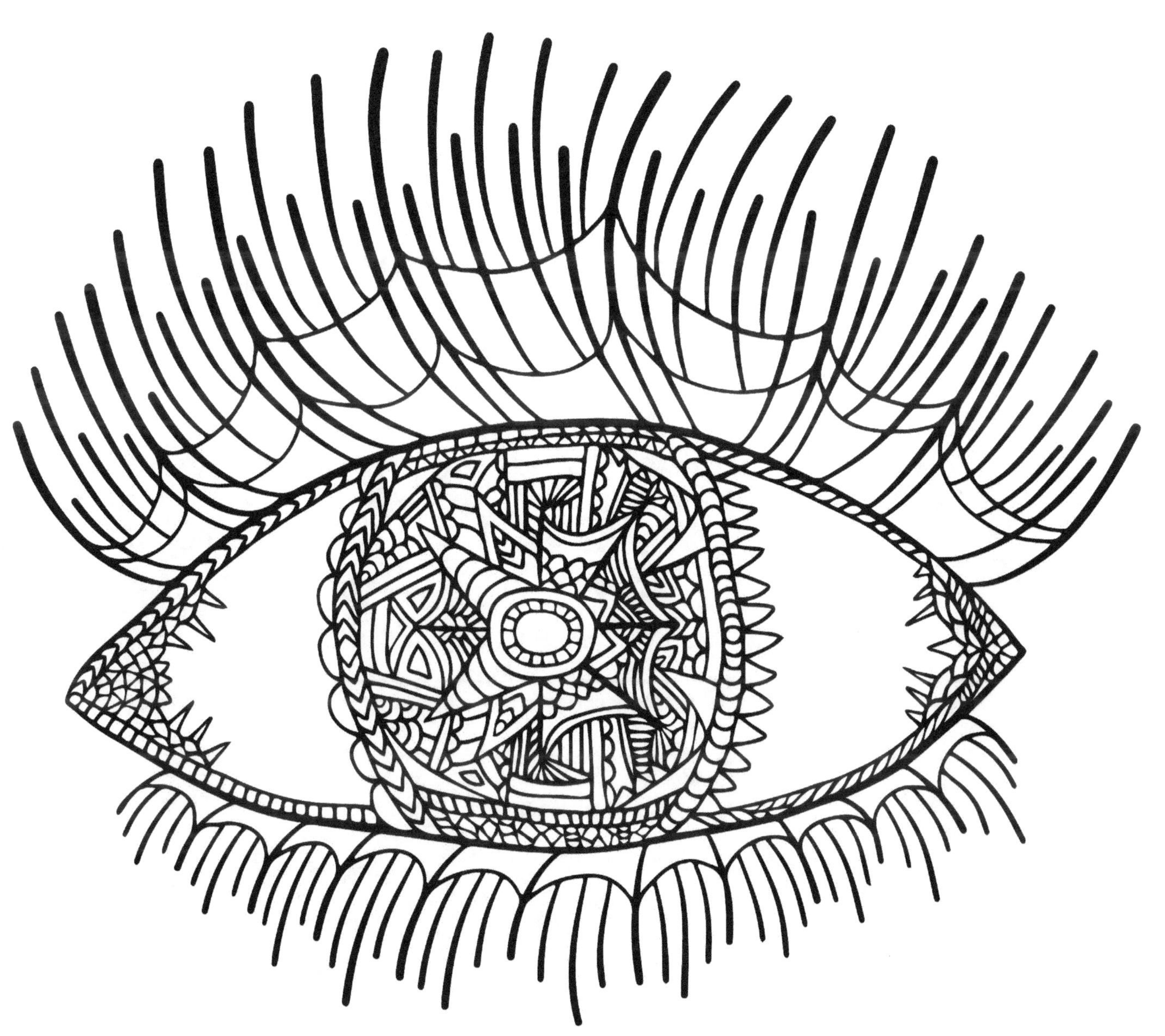

Forgiveness takes away what stands between
your brother and yourself.

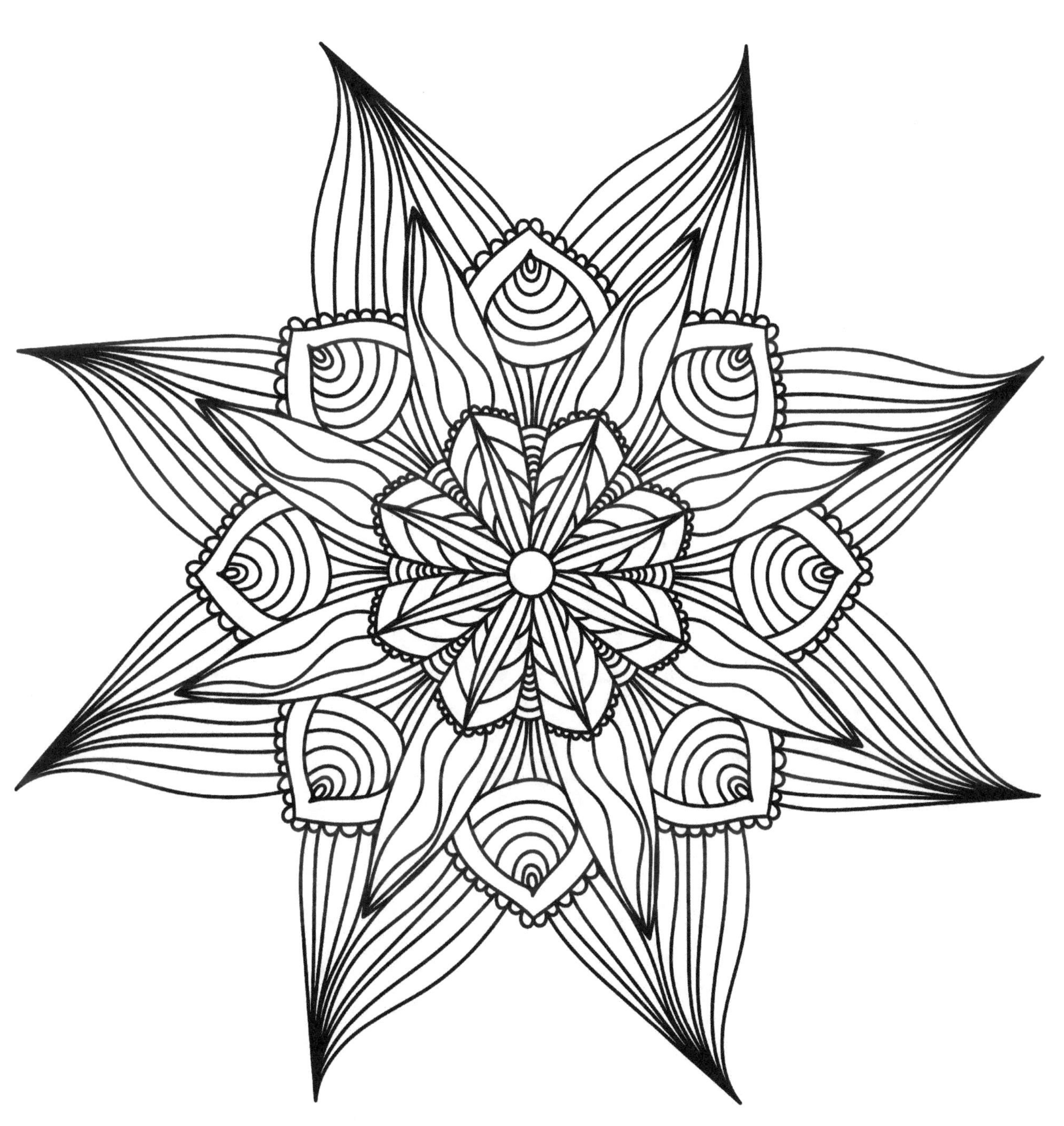

In the presence of truth, there are no unbelievers
and no sacrifices.

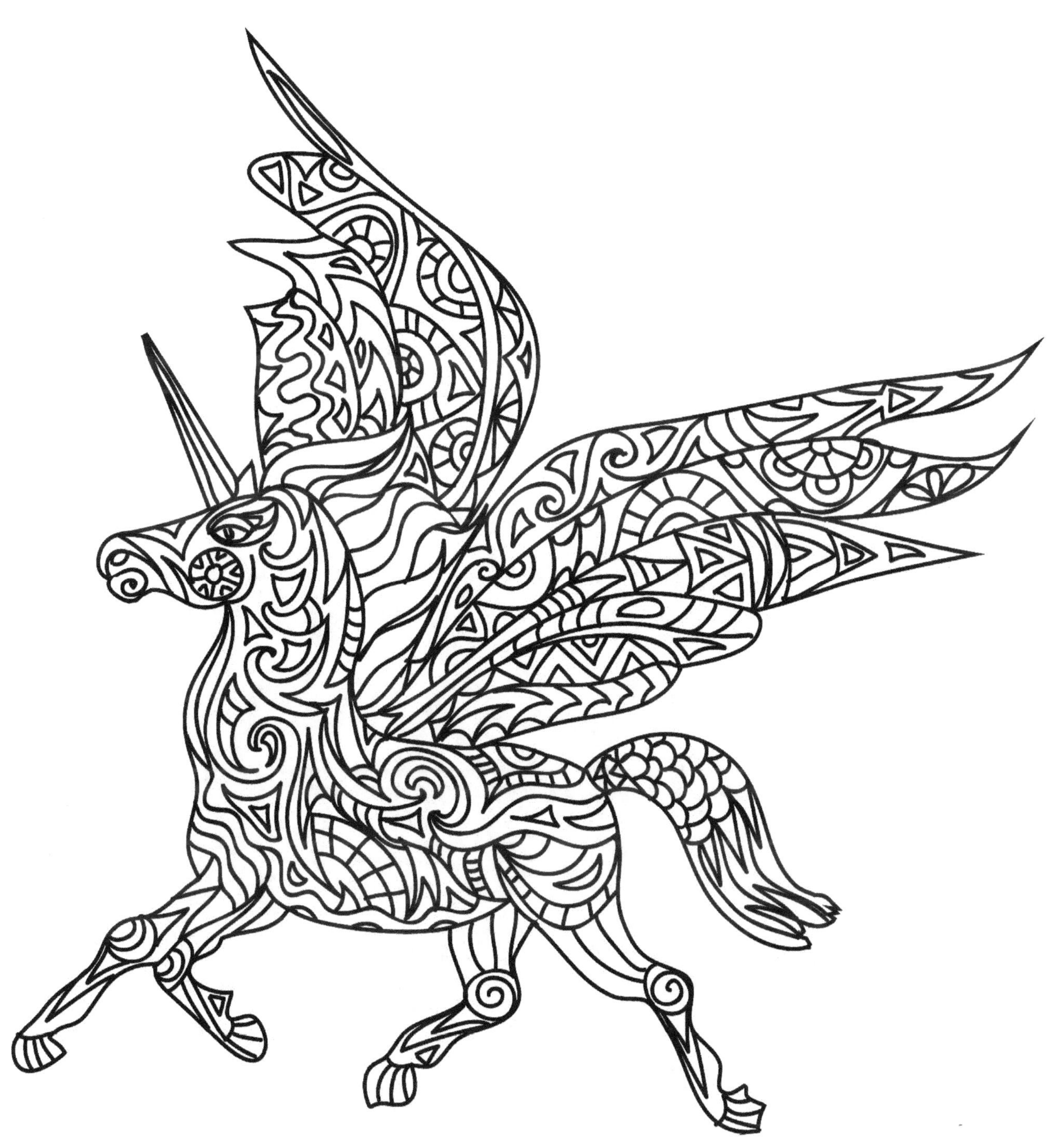

Judgement is not an attribute of God.

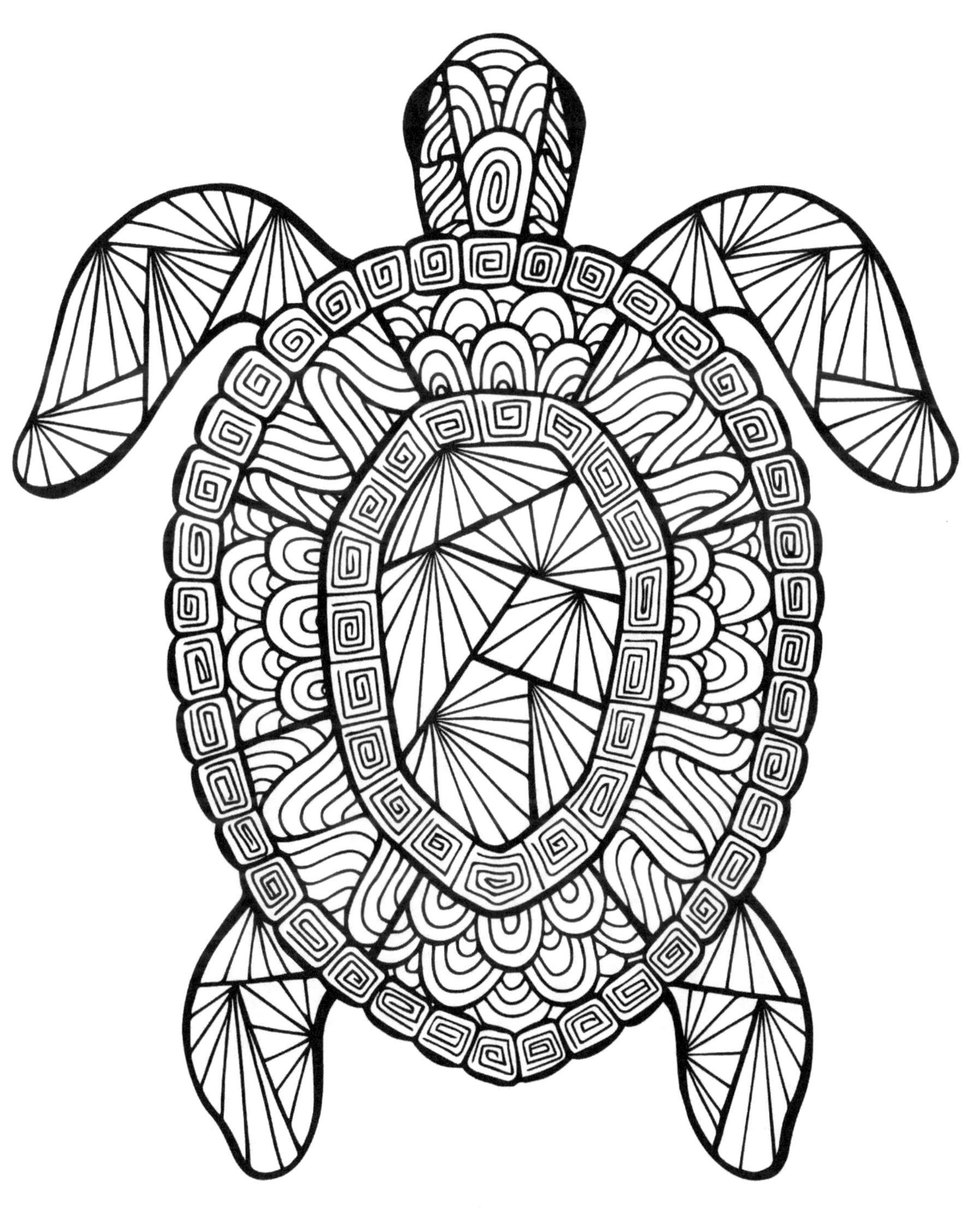

Where your heart is, there is your treasure also.
You believe in what you value.

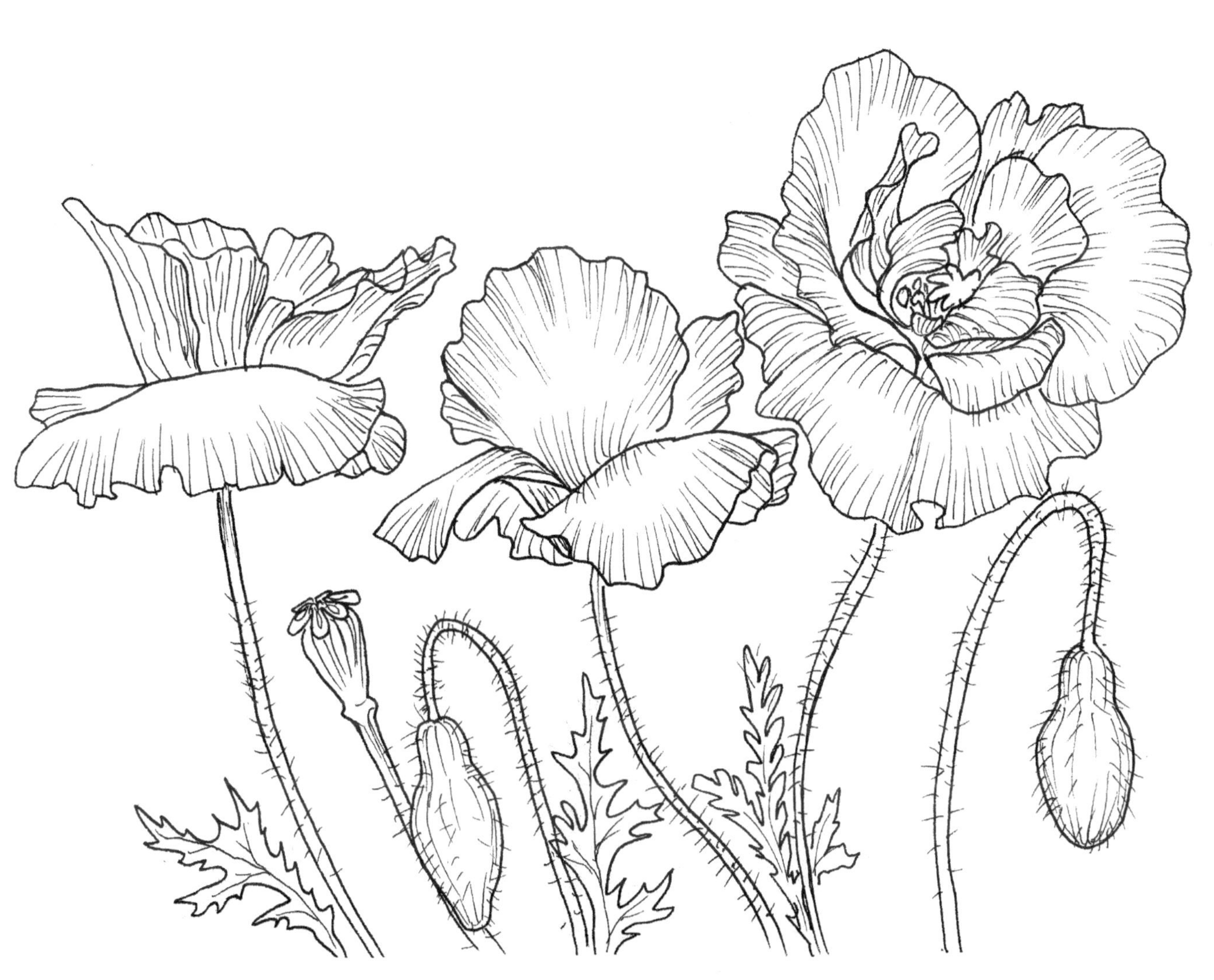

A sense of separation from God is the only lack
you really need correct.

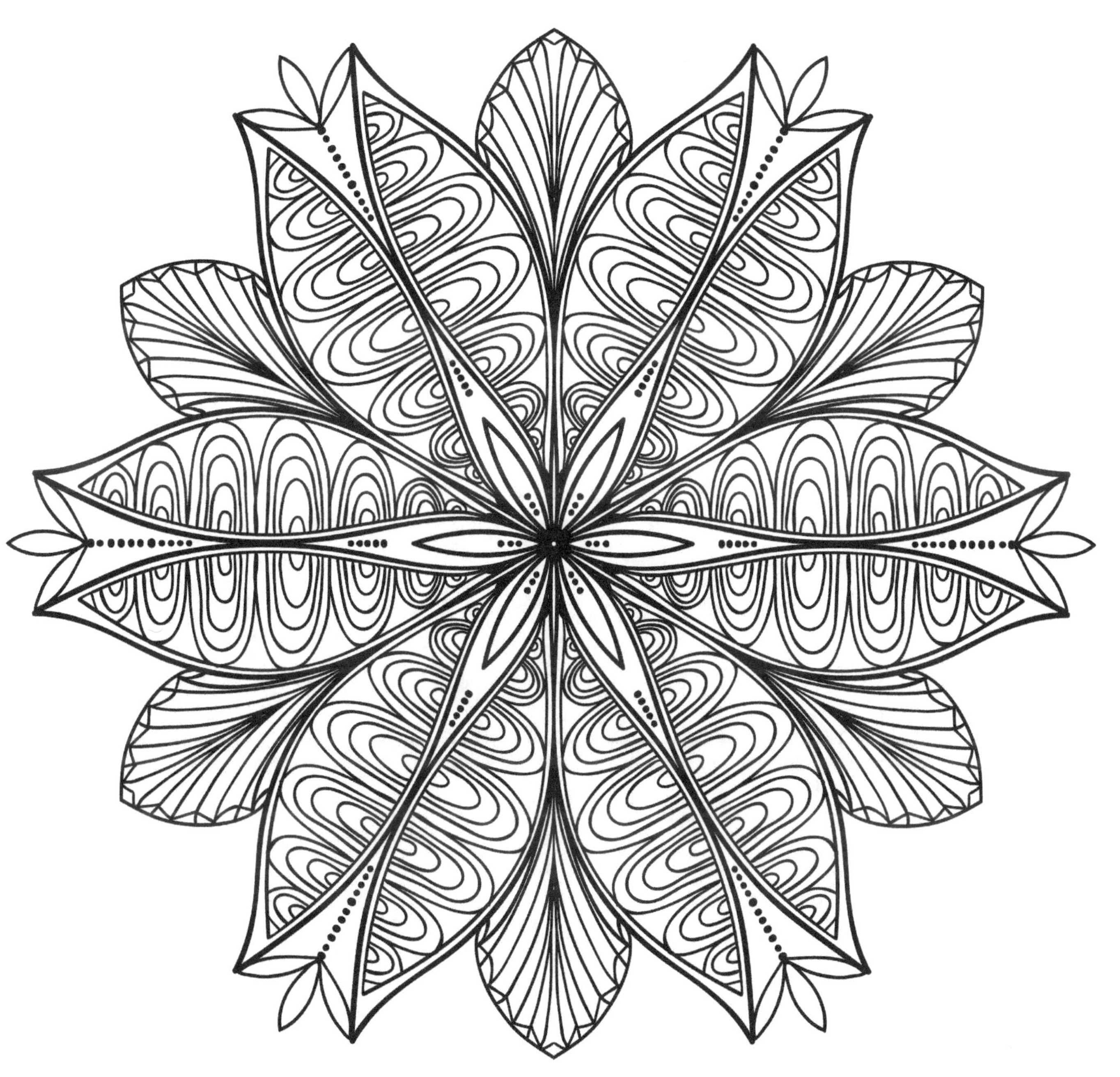

You have lost the knowledge that you yourself
are a miracle of God.

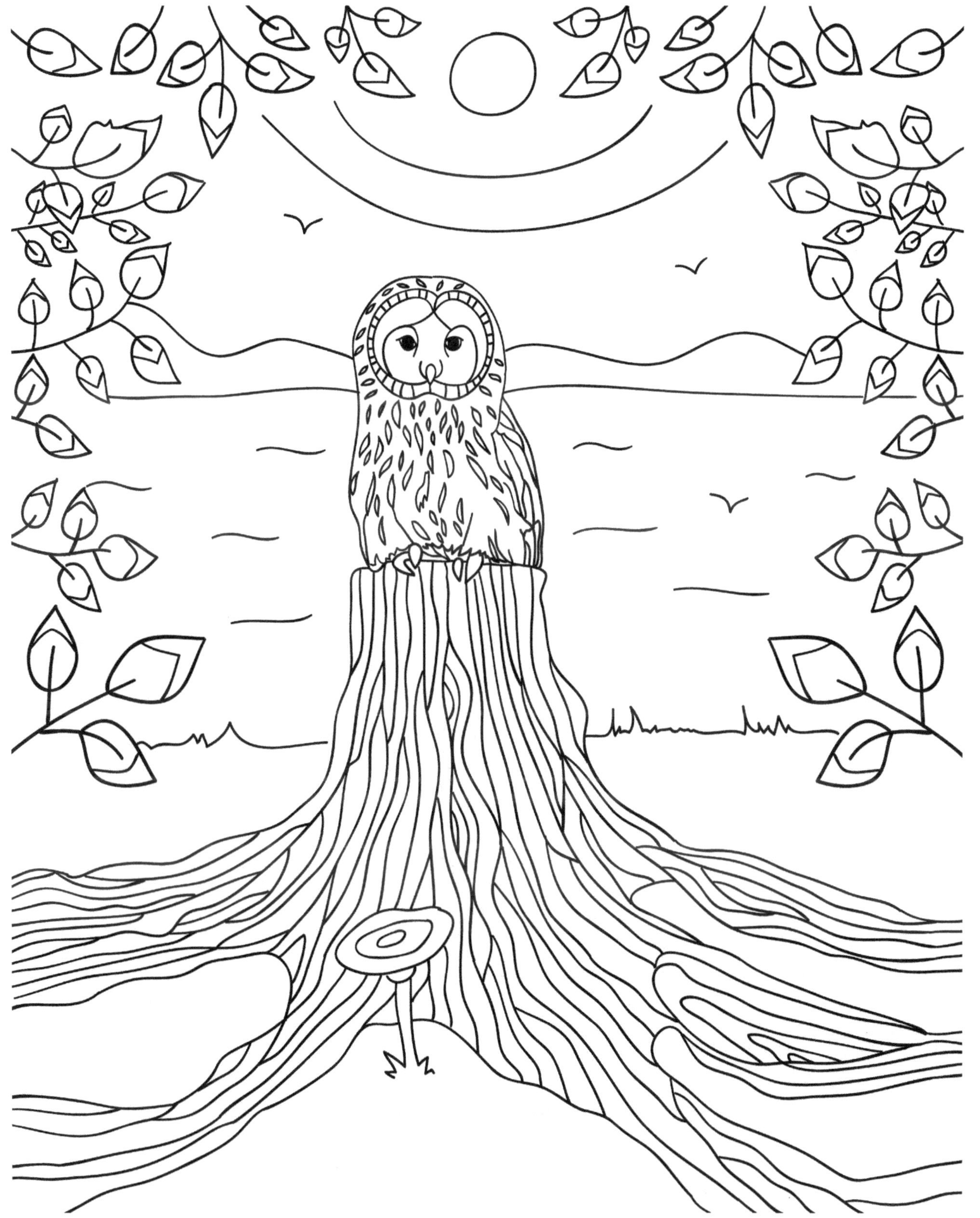

What can be more joyous than to perceive
we are deprived of nothing?

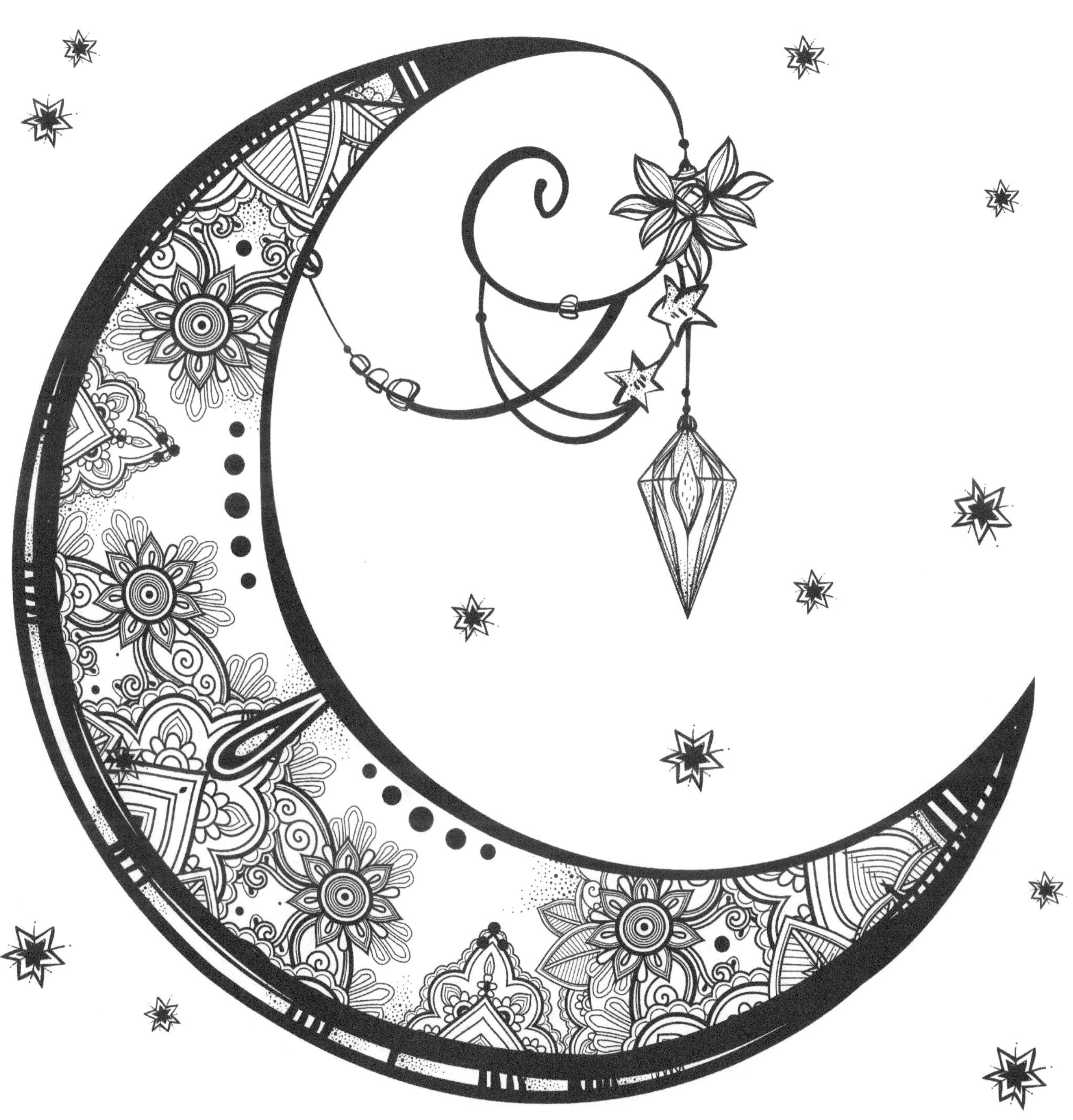

All your past except its beauty is gone,
and nothing is left but a blessing.

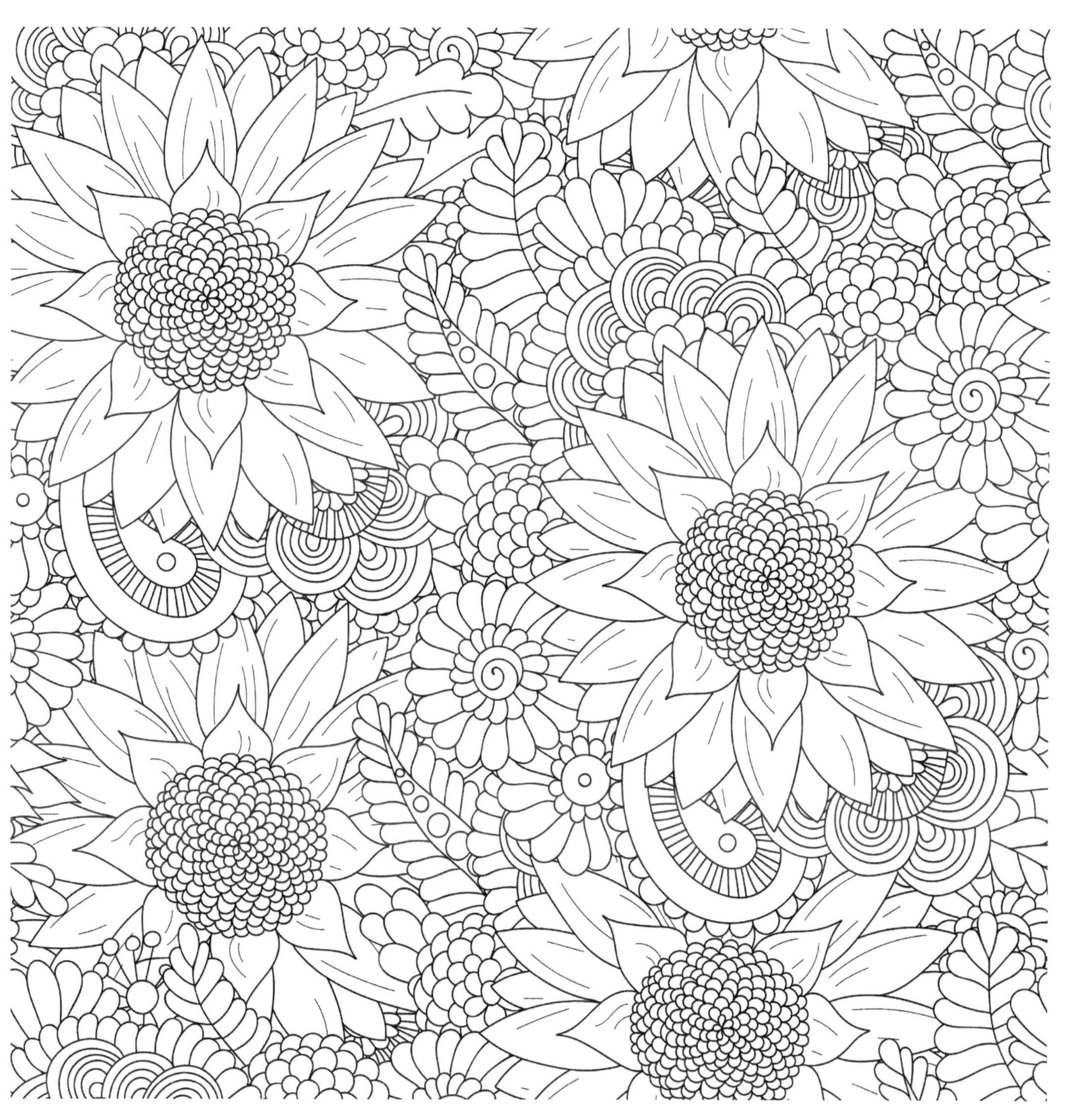

You who are part of God are not at home
except in His peace.

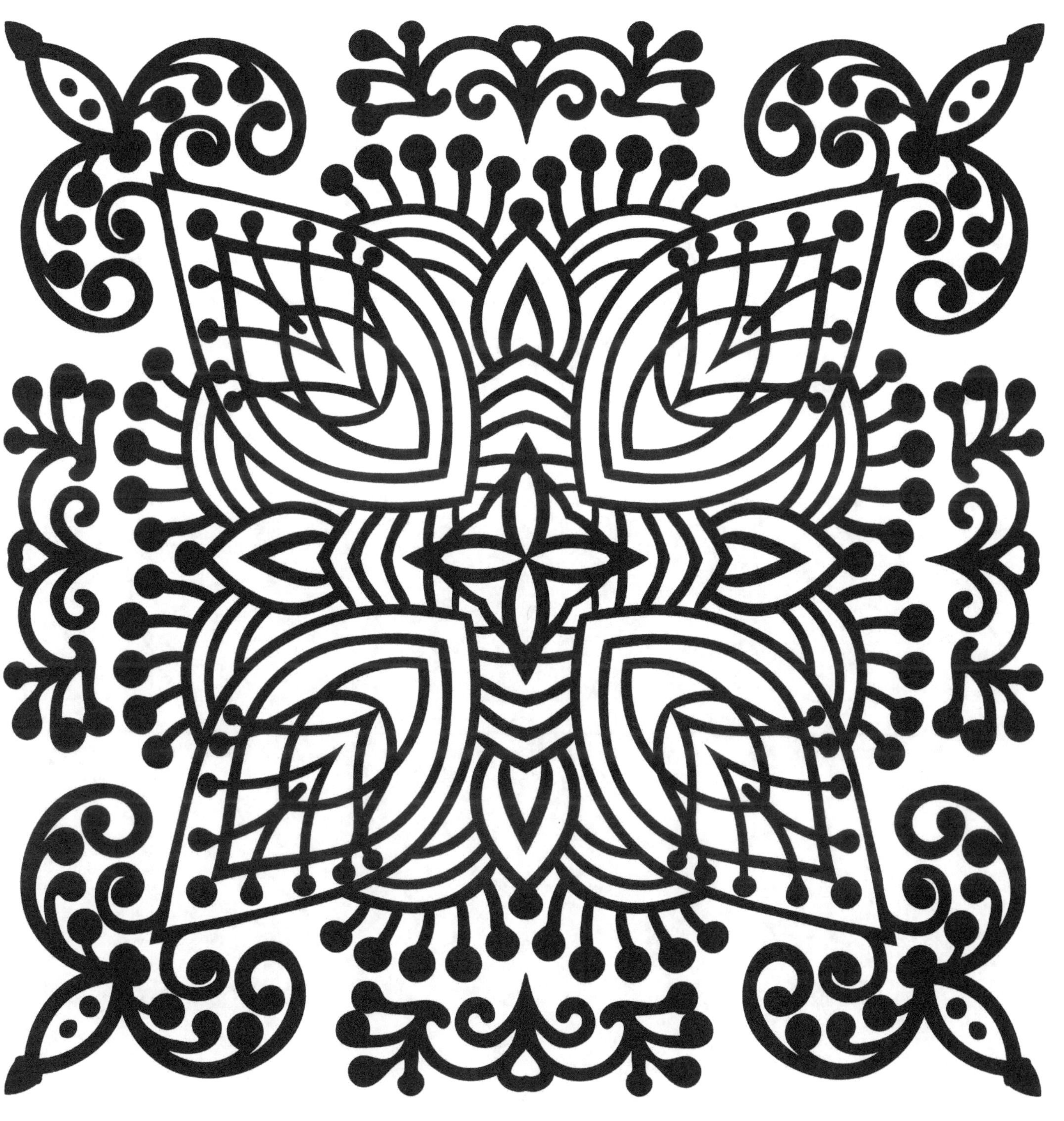

Peace is an attribute in you. You cannot find it outside.

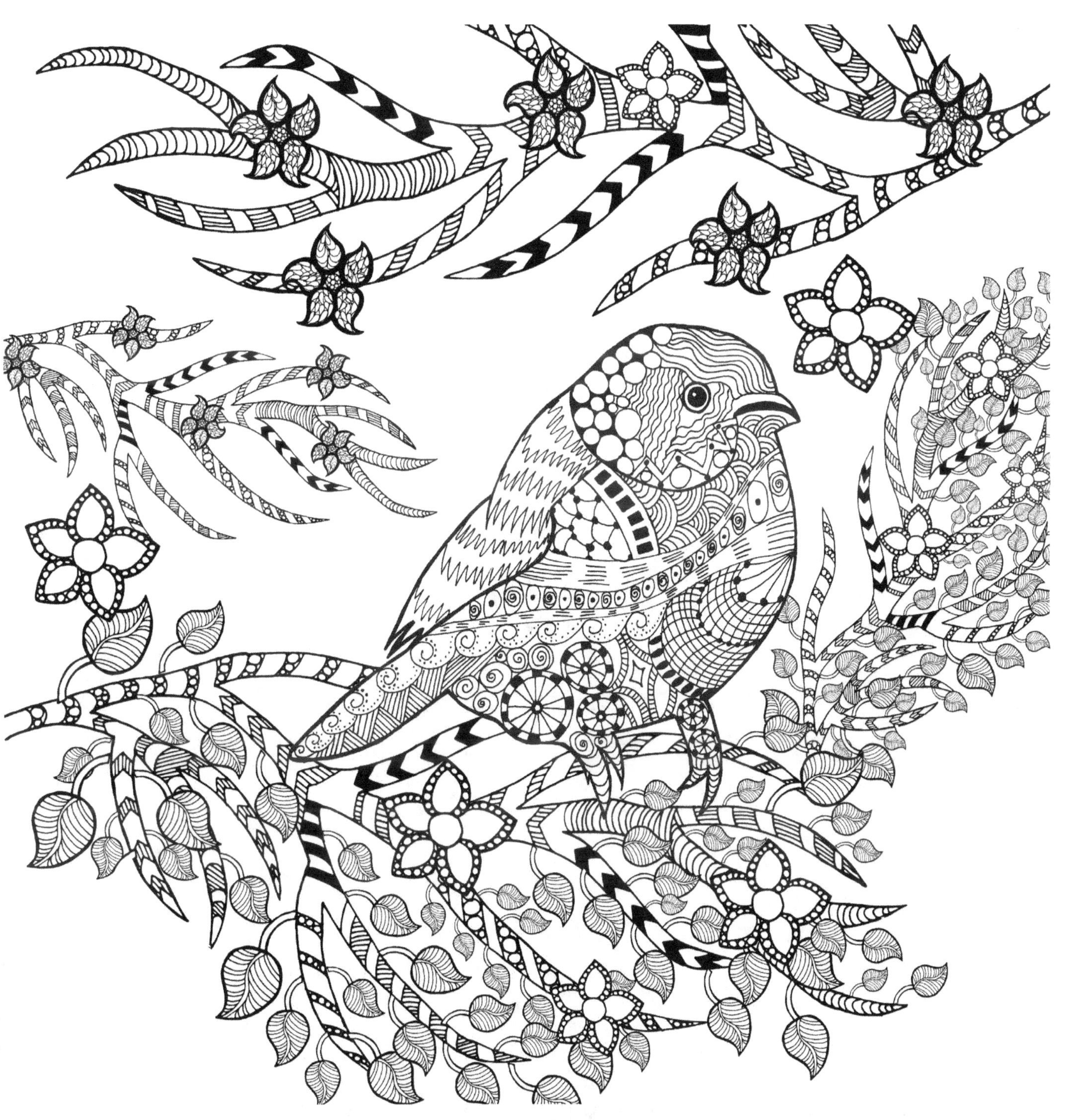

God has lit your mind Himself, and keeps your mind lit by His light because His light is what your mind is.

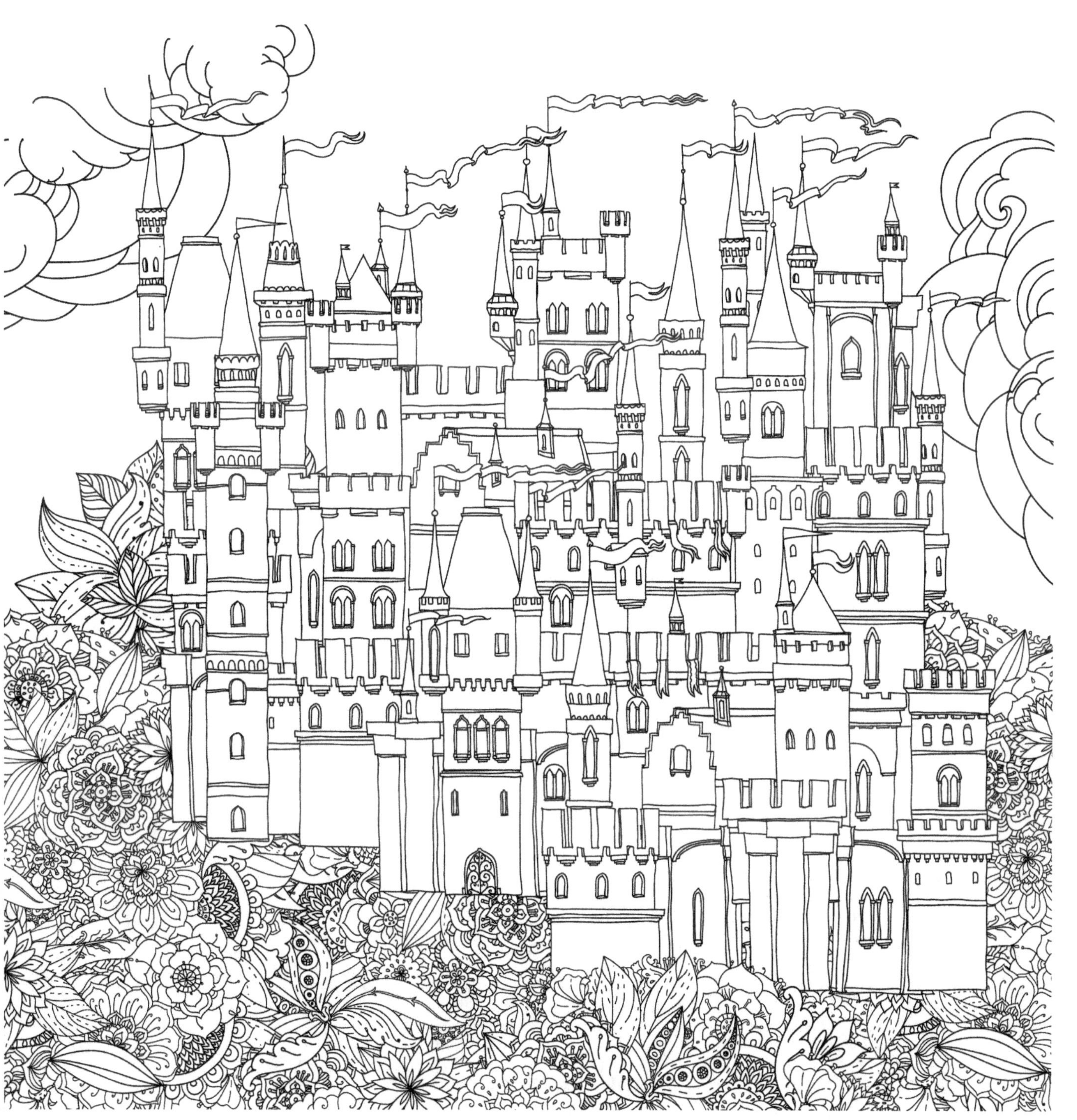

You cannot know your own perfection

until you have honored all those who were created like you.

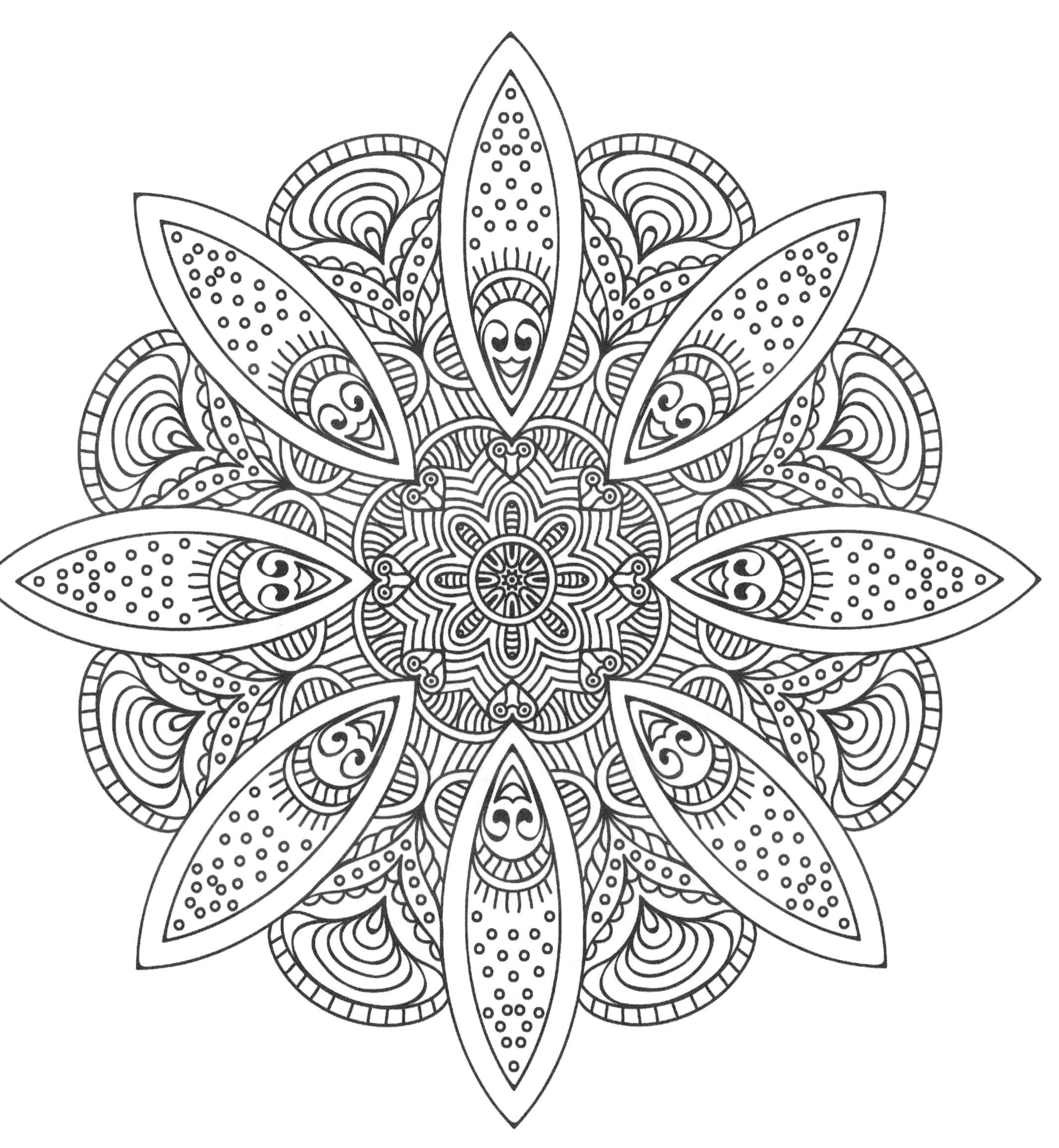

There is no time, no place, no state where God is absent.

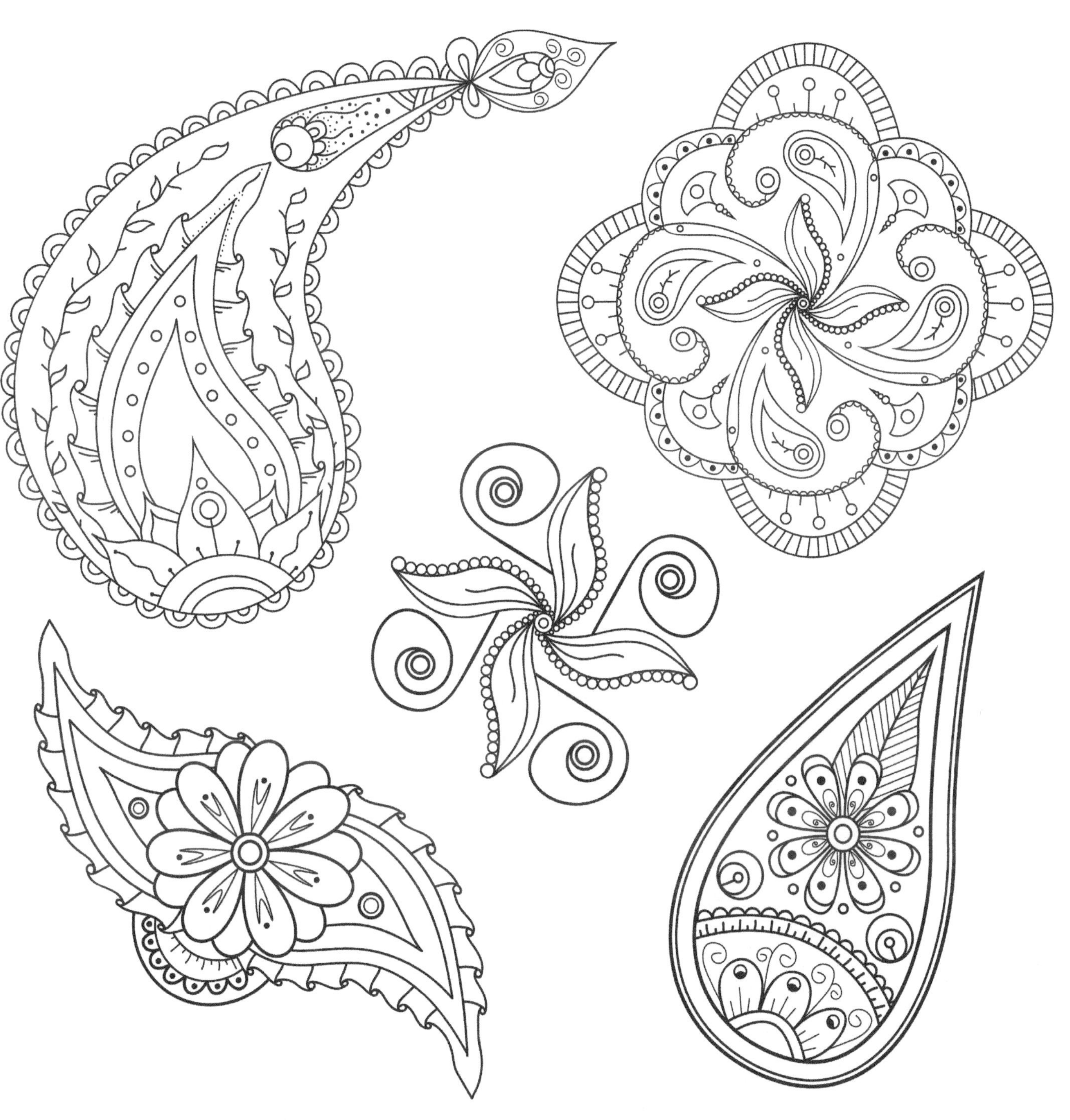

Beauty will rise to bless your sight
as you look upon the world with forgiving eyes.

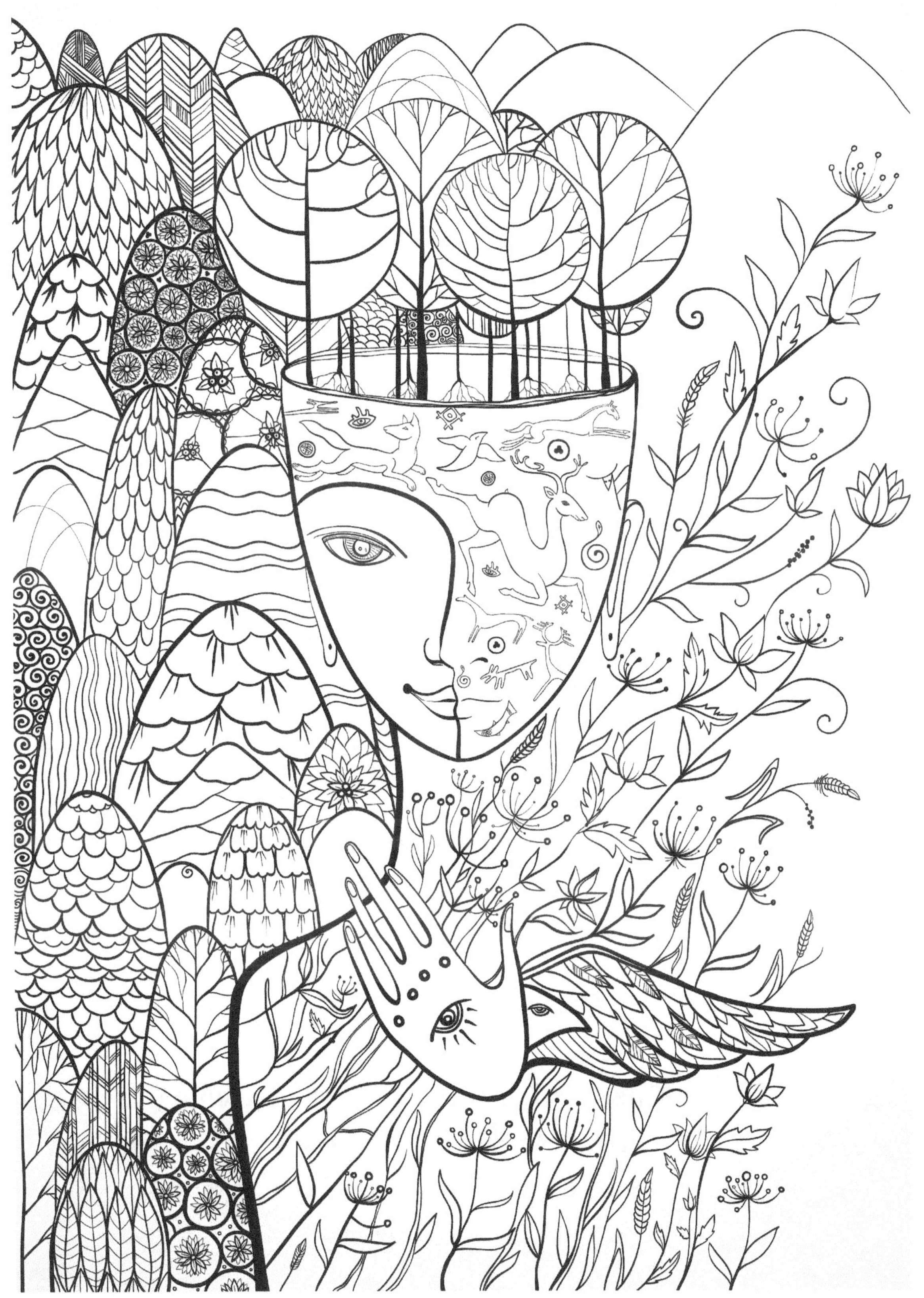

The journey to God is merely the reawakening
of the knowledge of where you are always, and what
you are forever. It is a journey without distance
to a goal that has never changed.

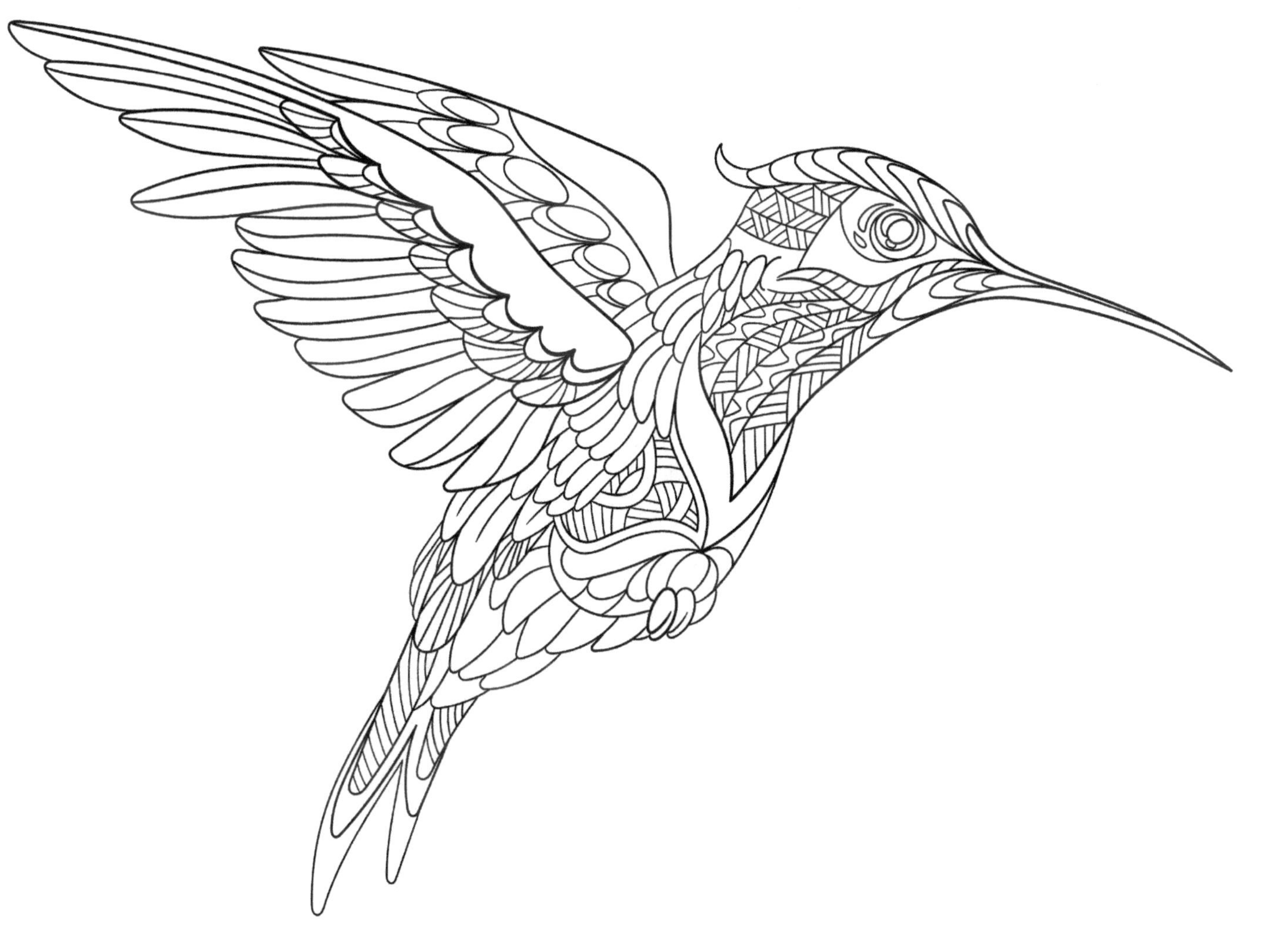

www.ingramcontent.com/pod-product-compliance
Lightning Source LLC
LaVergne TN
LVHW080930120826
845149LV00019B/1597

* 9 7 8 0 9 8 9 4 9 1 2 3 5 *